PRAISE FOR

Gehlek Rimpoche and *Good Life, Good Death*

"Gehlek's book is lighthearted and down-to-earth."
—*The Cleveland Plain Dealer*

"His teachings are helpful to all." —*The Denver Post*

"Insightful . . . Gehlek is a felicitous writer, especially gifted with analogy. Readers will cheer about this fresh voice."
—*Publishers Weekly* (starred review)

"Gehlek Rimpoche's wisdom on life, death and reincarnation will focus your energies on the importance of coming to terms with your negative emotions. It will also help you travel well through life by practicing patience." —*Spirituality & Health*

"Gehlek Rimpoche's mix of astute psychological insight, extraordinary intellect, and great compassion—plus his delightful wit—make him a wonderful, wise spiritual friend and guide."
—Tara Bennett-Goleman, author of *Emotional Alchemy*,
and Daniel Goleman, author of *Emotional Intelligence*

"Gehlek Rimpoche is a heartfelt, tender teacher with a vast analytic mind." —Allen Ginsberg

"Gehlek Rimpoche . . . is a great teacher."
—Robert A. F. Thurman,
professor of religion, Columbia University

"No clichés here. Just straight talk infused with humor, humility and a well-seasoned wisdom born of a broad classical training and worldly experience. His lineage is impeccable and true. His simple words speak to the jewel in our hearts." —Richard Gere

"Gehlek Rimpoche is one of the wisest, most cheerful people I know. He is a beautiful and gracious spirit who carries the great wisdom of Tibet. We are fortunate to have him teaching in the West." —Jack Kornfield,
bestselling author of *After the Ecstasy, the Laundry*

continued . . .

GOOD LIFE, GOOD DEATH

GEHLEK RIMPOCHE

WITH GINI ALHADEFF
AND MARK MAGILL

Foreword by
His Holiness the Dalai Lama

RIVERHEAD BOOKS
NEW YORK

RIVERHEAD BOOKS
Published by The Berkley Publishing Group
A division of Penguin Putnam Inc.
375 Hudson Street
New York, New York 10014

"Do the Meditation Rock," from *White Shroud: Poems 1980–1985* © 1987 Allen Ginsberg, reprinted by permission of HarperCollins Publishers.
"Gone, Gone, Gone," from *Death & Fame: Last Poems 1993–1997* © 1999 Allen Ginsberg, reprinted by permission of HarperCollins Publishers.

First Riverhead hardcover edition: October 2001
First Riverhead trade paperback edition: October 2002
Riverhead trade paperback ISBN: 1-57322-952-0

The Library of Congress has catalogued
the Riverhead hardcover edition as follows:

Nawang Gehlek, Rimpoche.
Good life, good death : Tibetan wisdom on reincarnation /
Rimpoche Nawang; with the help of Gini Alhadeff
and Mark Magill.
p. cm.
ISBN 1-57322-196-1
1. Reincarnation—Buddhism. 2. Death—Religious aspects—
Buddhism. 3. Future life—Buddhism. 4. Buddhism—China—
Tibet—Doctrines. I. Title.
BQ4485 .N39 2001   2001041625
294.3'4237—dc21

Printed in the United States of America

15 14 13 12 11

To my parents for giving me

such a wonderful life

And to my masters for helping me

learn how to live it

Contents

FOREWORD

Reincarnation is something we Tibetans tend to take for granted. We are brought up with the idea that the kind of life we have now is a result of how we have behaved in the past, and that the kind of life we will live in the future depends on how we conduct ourselves now. I feel this is in many ways a very practical approach because it places firmly in our own hands responsibility for the kind of person we are now and the kind of person we may become. What's more, it gives us a reason for making this very life as meaningful as possible. How should we go about doing this? I believe that cultivating compassion is one of the principal things that make our lives worthwhile. It is the source of all lasting happiness and joy. And it is the foundation of a good heart, the heart of one who acts out of a desire to help others.

Through kindness, through affection, through honesty, through truth, and through justice toward all others, we ensure our own benefit. This is not a matter for complicated theorizing. It is a matter of common sense. Consideration of others is worthwhile, because our happiness is inextricably bound up with the happiness of others. If society suffers, we ourselves suffer. And it is clear that the more our hearts and minds are afflicted with ill will, the more miserable we become. We cannot escape the necessity of love and compassion. As long as we have compassion for others and conduct ourselves with restraint—out of a sense of responsibility—there is no doubt we will be happy.

Of course, confidence in the way we have lived our lives is also one of the principal factors that will help us to remain calm and undisturbed at the time of death. The more we have made our lives meaningful, the less we will regret at the time of death. Therefore, the way we feel when we come to die is very much dependent on the way we have lived. If our daily life has been positive and meaningful, when the end comes, even though we do not wish for it, we will be able to accept it as a part of our life. We will have no regrets.

Nawang Gehlek Rimpoche has made these questions the theme of this book *Good Life, Good Death*. He is well qualified to discuss them. As a recognized reincar-

nate lama, he completed his traditional Buddhist training as a monk in Tibet prior to the Chinese takeover. In
exile in India, he lived the life of a married man, doing
valuable work in broadcasting and publishing Tibetan
Buddhist texts. Since becoming an American resident,
he has been able to put his clear understanding of the
English language and the modern world to good effect
when invited to teach about his own tradition. As this
book makes clear, he is able to share some of the in-
sights and benefits of the teachings of Tibetan Buddhism
with modern readers in terms that they can easily understand and put into practice. I am sure that readers interested in the Tibetan approach to inner peace will find
much here to attract and inspire them.

—*Tenzin Gyatso,*
The Fourteenth Dalai Lama
June 16, 2001

INTRODUCTION

Over the years, I have probably had more fun with Gehlek Rimpoche than with almost any lama I have known. Extremely bright and perceptive, he has a great sense of humor, and just loves to chat, whether in Tibetan or English. He is also very good-natured and generous to a fault, not minding at all when the joke's on him. I have also learned a great deal from him, about all levels of the Buddha Dharma, which he lives and breathes. It's in his mind as a philosophy, in his culture as a way of life, and in his blood as an art of living and dying well—that is, virtuously for the sake of others and pleasantly for his own sake.

Rimpoche was brought up in one of the most upper-crust families in Tibet, belonging to the family of the Great Thirteenth Dalai Lama, Thubten Gyatso (1876–1933), the "first family" of that era—sort of like the Roosevelts in America. His father was also an important reincarnation. In spite of his father's effort to have Gehlek Rimpoche lead a more normal life, his son was recognized as the reincarnation of an important lama.

So at an early age, Gehlek Rimpoche had to leave his comfortable and stimulating home for the relatively harsh life of the formal training of an incarnate lama. As a novice monk, he underwent a rigorous intellectual, spiritual, and moral education. He had to spend long hours memorizing hundreds of pages of profound and difficult texts, almost hopelessly abstruse and boring for a young boy. If he failed in a particular day's recitation, he would be soundly beaten, forced to stay awake and make up the lesson, though fortunately he was so intelligent, he could memorize over a dozen pages at a sitting, hundreds of verses, even though he didn't know the meaning of most of them. He tells a story, backed up by schoolmates whom I also know, about how he used to frustrate his tutors by learning his verses so well that he could keep on reciting them accurately even while having fallen asleep, thus satisfying his memorization quota while also getting some rest. So upset that he was getting out of his duties, they made him recite while standing up on the windowsill of his third-story study room, thinking that the fear of falling would keep him awake. He responded by learning to sleep standing up, leaning slightly against the window frame. Finally, they had to back down for fear he really might fall.

During his late childhood and adolescence he began to learn the meaning of the library of teachings he had memorized, and he became the talk of his college—the Loseling College of Drepung monastery, with over ten thousand monks the largest monastic university in the world—for his quickness in penetration, sharpness in analytic debate, elegance in ritual performance, and depth of understanding. Tibetan monks normally do not engage in contemplation in groups, unlike Zen monks, but rather meditate in solitude in their own quarters, using meditation to complete the process of developing wisdom through broad learning by memorizing the root texts and studying the commentaries with a teacher, and then debating with classmates in fiercely competitive formal analysis to bring out the deeper meanings. Rimpoche was a terror on the debating court, and thus he advanced through the stages of his studies with re-markable speed.

He also soon became the protégé of some of the most important lamas of the day, particularly Lingtsang and Trijang Rimpoches, the senior and junior tutors of His Holiness the Dalai Lama, who were most eminently qualified to transmit the esoteric precepts and inner-most contemplative empowerments of the advanced Vajrayana teachings.

There is no question that Gehlek Rimpoche received the best education possible in his time and circumstances: the rod was not spared and he was not spoiled. He totally excelled in all his studies and practices and graduated in record time. He also did have a little bit of down-time at home with his family, and since his father was not only a member of high society but also a notable psychic and even a kind of oracle, he got to know all the important people in Lhasa during the forties and fifties and so knew something about the world of Tibet and its society, including all the wrenching changes that were taking place due to the invasion of the communist Chinese during the years leading up to the 1959 escape of His Holiness the Dalai Lama.

In 1959, Rimpoche's world was shattered. The communist Chinese became impatient with maintaining the pretense of compromising their principles to accommodate a Buddhist culture, society, and government and made a grab for total control. Hundreds of thousands of Tibetans were massacred and imprisoned, the Dalai Lama and many of his key monastic and lay officials escaped, monasteries were destroyed, many monks died by gunfire, and many more perished in the wilderness during the arduous crossing of the Himalayas while fleeing into exile into India, Nepal, Bhutan, and Sikkim. Like the Dalai Lama, Rimpoche had barely graduated when he nearly lost his life. He did, indeed, lose his monastery, many of his teachers and classmates, his family, his society, his country, his most cherished possessions, and his entire Tibetan Buddhist civilization. It would be hard to imagine a more powerful lesson in impermanence, suffering, and alienation.

After many adventures of escape, relocation, and establishing himself in exile along with a hundred thousand other Tibetan refugees, Rimpoche rebelled against his whole former lifestyle. He resigned his monk's vows. He married. He visited America and learned English well, and then took a job in a big city, New Delhi, capital of the newly independent India. He also took up responsibility for his devastated country, going to work for Tibet House in New Delhi, H. H. the Dalai Lama's initial cultural center, established in order to catch and preserve some of the seeds of Tibetan civilization that were being scattered on the winds of history. He entered a new phase of his education, learning about the larger world, about Indians and Westerners, about Hindus and Christians and Jews, and secular humanists and atheists. He learned about all these people by being one among them, a refugee with no special status. He became a man of the world—though privately, in spite of the many doubts that arose due to the utter catastrophe his world had suffered, he maintained his practices.

I began to get to know Rimpoche during this period. I was a year or two younger, a New Yorker who had had plenty of fun in prep school and college, and I was already married once, with a young daughter. I was rebelling in the opposite direction and had become a wandering philosopher and seeker of enlightenment. Unaware of the full horror of what was going on in Tibet, I was immersing myself in Tibet-in-exile, becoming a monk, beginning a much lesser version of the education Rimpoche had just finished. Going in opposite directions, we had an immediate rapport. During the various phases of my progress forth and back through the '60s and '70s in Delhi and America, Rimpoche was always kind, generous, knowledgeable, and helpful to me. My main teachers were his main teachers, and so I didn't really see him as a teacher in those days. Then from the late '70s, when I got to spend more time in India doing research into the Vajrayana yogas, I began to study with Rimpoche directly, and my appreciation of his depth increased immensely. He knew everything I wanted to know, and yet he maintained a worldly, friendly relationship, explaining things not only from his classical education but also from his experience in the world. His teachers, especially Lingtsang Rimpoche, had begun to push him again, to urge him to take up his responsibilities as a Dharma teacher. I was impressed by how highly they regarded him, and so I invited him to teach in America, at our little Institute of Buddhist Studies in Amherst, Massachusetts, and other places. Having received formal teachings from his teachers— some of the greatest lamas of the previous generation— I can truly say that Rimpoche carries their message in a complete and authentic way, and, even more interesting, he enfolds it in an envelope of contemporary savvy, from his wide experience of people from all over the world, knowing where they're coming from, what they want, and what they need.

What I like about Rimpoche is that he has consistently shown resiliency and flexibility of character. I have also seen in him signs of a sound understanding of selflessness, the hallmark Buddhist teaching. He can be an elegant lama in the formal setting, a truly worthy representative of his illustrious lineage. He can be a wise advisor in another setting, placing responsibility for growth where it belongs: on the individual. He can be a loyal and creative colleague, in the endless work of seeing to the long duration and continuing usefulness of the Dharma. Throughout it all, he remains a cherished and jolly person, a good friend.

I welcome *Good Life, Good Death* of this good friend, which contains much wise advice and practical suggestions for contemporary people—how to get more out of this life, while having more fun in the bargain.

—*Robert A. F. Thurman*
Ganden Dekyiling, Woodstock, New York
July 4, 2001

AUTHOR'S NOTE

My name is Nawang Gehlek Trinley Namgye. My reincarnation title is Nyare Khentul. "Rimpoche" is an hon-
orific used to refer to reincarnated lamas. I say this
because some people think all Rimpoches are members
of the same family. Rimpoche means "Precious One."
Incarnate lamas are supposed to have taken rebirth by
choice, for the benefit of all. Such persons are rare and
important, and that's why they're called precious. I happen to have received this status, but I have no such qualities as taking rebirth by choice and commitment as far
as I know or can remember.

Why should you listen to me about reincarnation?
No reason, really. I speak from personal experience,
from sixty years of personal experience and study. I'm
not inventing anything new. What I have to say is based
on the experience of the Buddha, which dates back
2,500 years and was passed down in an unbroken line to

my masters. I learned from the tried, tested, reliable, and authentic words of their masters before them.

Talking, teaching, and consoling are the duties of an incarnate lama, and I think I'm trying to fulfill them. The greatest example is His Holiness the Dalai Lama.

What I have learned may help you ease your pain, relax your anxieties, reduce your anger, reduce your attachment, and build a little wisdom. It is nothing that you don't already know. I say it to remind you and to remind myself that within each of us we have every solution to our problems.

One

WHO ARE WE?

When I first came to the United States, I hesitated to talk about reincarnation because I thought people wouldn't like it or be able to understand it. I was afraid they'd think it was some kind of fairy tale or plain religious brainwashing. But when I finally did talk about it, to my surprise, people nodded their heads in agreement, as though they accepted and liked the idea. I began to wonder what made them like it. Why did they accept it so easily when someone like me, who was supposed to be a reincarnated lama and had spent a whole life trying to comprehend it, still had a hard time accepting it? Why did a group of Americans sitting down to listen to a stranger from Tibet talking about reincarnation find it so simple and easy to accept?

That was a big question for me. I thought about it and talked to a number of people. I realized they were drawn to reincarnation because it's "mystical." Maybe they thought that through reincarnation they'd be able to go back to being the same people they were with a full knowledge of their previous lives. I suspect that's why many accepted it without knowing what it was. An attachment to the idea that one might continue to exist made it easy to accept, at least in word, if not in understanding.

So what's the catch? As I understand it, there's a big surprise. The surprise is that the continuity of an individual is very, very subtle. Memories are usually later. The individual's life does not continue as such. Reincarnation can be an uncontrolled, crazy whirlwind in which we are blown about like autumn leaves not knowing where we're going to be dropped.

One of Buddha's chief disciples, a monk called Mahakatyayana, was walking through a forest with a group of students. They came upon a lake where a man, a woman, and their baby were eating a fish they had just caught. Their dog was barking and begging for food.

On catching sight of them, Mahakatyayana stopped and burst out laughing. Everyone wanted to know why. He explained, "In a former life, the baby the mother now holds to her breast was a man her husband murdered for having assaulted her. The fish they are eating was the baby's grandfather and the dog begging for a piece of that fish was his grandfather's wife."

Continuations

We wonder who we are, where we come from, where we are going, and how we get there. These are not new questions. Twenty-five hundred years ago, Buddha was asked where and when we began and whether or not there would be an end to our taking rebirth. Buddha's answer was silence, because the beginning cannot be pinpointed.

There is no new consciousness born, and no consciousness is ever destroyed. All consciousness resurfaces somehow. That's why we continue to go from life to life, all of us, the same beings, from the limitless beginning of time. That's the basis of the Buddhist notion that every sentient being has been your mother. This may be a controversial statement, and I can't prove it scientifically. In fact, it's as difficult to prove as reincarnation. But that's the basic premise of reincarnation: No new consciousness is born; everyone is endlessly circling around from birth to death, birth to death.

Every consciousness that already exists will always exist. And every consciousness has the potential to become fully enlightened, to have total freedom from negative emotions as well as their imprints—to be faultless in qualities and knowledge.

Consciousness changes its physical identity all the time. For the most part, identifying who is who is a little difficult because the changes between one life and the next are drastic.

That everybody is a reincarnation was Buddha's realization. In my culture, pre-communist Tibet, we developed a system for recognizing certain beings, known as incarnate lamas, who keep coming back for a specific purpose. They are called *tulkus*—"tul" means manifestation and "ku" means form. Tulkus are supposed to be special in that they are free of negative emotions and can help others to be free.

The system of tulkus, or recognized reincarnations, began with the first Karmapa, about five centuries after the introduction of Buddhism in Tibet. Up through the sixteenth reincarnation of the Karmapa, who died in the early 1980s, each reincarnation left letters announcing who the next reincarnation would be. Soon, reincarnations of the Dalai Lama, the Panchen Lama, and thousands of others were identified. And, in some cases, multiple reincarnations of the same tulku were discovered. At the enlightened level, the possibility of manifestation is unlimited.

To highly developed lamas, past and future lives are as ordinary as yesterday and tomorrow. They sometimes talk among themselves about a future life as if they were making plans for the next day. I was told the story of a famous lama with a big nose who had Parkinson's disease. One day, His Holiness the Fourteenth Dalai Lama noticed the man was shaking very violently, so he said to him, "I am not going to tell you the usual things, to have a long life, and continue to help all beings, but when I see a young boy who tells me, 'I am the one with the big nose,' I'll be happy to recognize him as your reincarnation." The lama went home very relieved to have had that conversation, and within a short time, he died.

There are different ways by which tulkus are recognized. One is based on self-identification, a tulku revealing his or her identity even at a very early age. As soon as the second Dalai Lama was born in the sixteenth century, he opened his big round eyes, turned them in the direction of Tashi Lunpo, the monastery of the first Dalai Lama, and started praying. He recited mantras as soon as he could talk, and when he was about three and his mother scolded him, he sang a song to her saying, "I will not stay here: I have a much better house with many more rooms in Tashi Lunpo." His mother was curious: "Where do you come from?" she asked. He told her, "When I died, as they tied my body with ropes to take me to the place where sky burials are performed, I saw the six-armed protector Mahakala wearing metal shoes and his mask of fierceness. I went with him and this is where he led me." He named the man who had tied his old body. Later, when he was seven, he recognized the old man who had been his attendant at the monastery and bestowed on him the blessing of Zambala, who is the god of wealth. The old man started crying.

A common system of recognizing incarnations, by which even His Holiness the Fourteenth Dalai Lama was recognized, is to see if the candidate can recognize some of his or her predecessor's personal belongings, such as a rosary or a pair of glasses. Then the time of birth is another indication, both because there might have been oracles indicating when that would be and because the event itself might have been distinguished by some supernatural sign witnessed by several people, such as a rainbow appearing above the parents' house, or a spring flower born in the dead of winter. In one case, a raven perched on top of a prayer flag guarding the baby day and night for two years. Prophetic dreams and visions were very common, especially if more than one person could confirm having received the same message and if the choice was then confirmed by a respected clairvoyant lama. I know this may sound fantastic to Westerners, but for Tibetans it was and still is as normal as a weather forecast.

Some reincarnations of earlier masters receive no official recognition although a lot of people know who they are. Tashi Namgyal, an abbot whose reincarnation I was confirmed to be, was one such. But before that happened, I had a bumpy ride, thinking I might be the reincarnation of the Panchen Lama one minute and of someone else the next. Many search parties came to our house to see if I was the boy they were looking for. For the Panchen Lama interview, a huge party arrived at our house with twenty to thirty horses. I was only three, and I remember it looked like a big crowd to me. I liked the idea that I might be recognized as a very high-ranking lama such as the Panchen Lama, because that would have entitled me to a throne at least as big and high as my father's, who was not only an incarnate lama but born into the family of the thirteenth Dalai Lama. The fact that he was such a respected lama was what landed me on several lists.

When Tashi Namgyal died, the people of his institutions and his attendants gave away practically all of his wealth and belongings because they did not expect him to be reincarnated or recognized. They had just one little carpet and a small chest left by the time they were told to start looking for the reincarnation. They dragged their feet and hoped the matter would go away. My father lost no opportunity to say he didn't think I was an incarnate lama at all, though he also said I might in some way be connected to the Buddha of Light. He had serious doubts about the entire tulku system; he thought it was too vulnerable to political maneuverings and that it might have outlived its purpose.

One very respected Rimpoche said the reincarnation of Tashi Namgyal was likely to be the son of a prominent lama in Lhasa, and that pretty much pointed to me. My father did everything he could to block the process, even going so far as to say that he would give me up only if I were given a high ranking; he hoped that the government would reject the request without even taking it into consideration. But the man entrusted with finding the reincarnation of my predecessor became the regent of Tibet, and he took his task very seriously. To my father's great surprise, the ranking was granted, and I was confirmed at the age of four.

I was sent to live with my first teacher at a nearby retreat area, then I entered Drepung monastery at the age of five. At my welcoming ritual at the monastery, where I was to be educated, my teacher said, "I hope you complete your monastic studies as quickly as possible and remain in Lhasa to give teachings to hundreds of thousands of people." That I really was the reincarnation of an abbot named Tashi Namgyal was totally accepted. If it hadn't been totally accepted, they would have told me to be a good boy and not dreamed of asking a small child like me to teach thousands of people. The request made me see my responsibility to others very clearly, as well as what was expected of me. It created a solid guideline, a plan for my life.

I stayed at Drepung until I was nineteen, when I escaped from Tibet to India, where I remained a monk for a few more years.

When I was in my twenties and having a teenage rebellion, the doubt I had been entertaining since adolescence about reincarnation surfaced more strongly than ever. I read the biographies of the different incarnate lamas. Many of them contained recollections of their previous lives. But, when I tried to remember anything regarding my previous lives and circumstances, conditions and friends, my vivid, reliable recollections equaled zero. Then I wondered, What am I? A fool?

While living in Delhi during the 1960s and '70s, I suffered tremendously. When a friend of my family who was married to a man of royal descent from Ladakh died in Delhi, her father asked me to do a transference of consciousness for her. I hadn't done one for a long time and I did not have any of the necessary materials for the ritual, such as the mixture you put on the crown of the person's head. Besides, I had my doubts as to whether these rituals worked.

I went to the house at six in the evening. I sat alone with the woman's body and recited a long prayer very slowly, with all my concentration. When I got to the verses for transferring the consciousness, I gathered my thoughts on that very carefully and applied them to what I was doing. One of this woman's gurus was Bakula Rimpoche, who was a member of parliament in India at that time. The very next day, he told me that the deceased woman had come to "visit" him at about seven P.M., the exact time that I had transferred her consciousness to be united with the mind of enlightenment.

That confused me further, but it also weakened my doubts. It indicated to me that something was working, though I still didn't have perfect confirmation. Of course, I was not the only one there—other lamas were present—but I was alone with the body, and the timing seemed to indicate that what I was doing had some effect. I remember discussing my doubts with my teachers Ling and Trijang Rimpoche. They listened very kindly.

My understanding of reincarnation came gradually through a long process of learning from the great Buddhist teachers. Learning from the great Buddhist texts. Learning through debate, through meditation and practice. After all that, I can now say I have some kind of firm and unshakable belief in reincarnation.

It comes from a deeper consciousness that lies at the heart level, a kind of pervasive understanding. Not a voice, but a comprehension coming from inside rather than outside. That's why I believe in reincarnation—not only because Buddha said one should.

Some friends tell me that this is just Tibetan conditioning, but the same could be said for the Western lack of belief in reincarnation. In Tibet, we saw or heard of small children resuming conversations with adults right where they had been left off in previous lifetimes, performing religious rituals they couldn't possibly know, or insisting they lived in houses in distant cities they had never been to, with people they had never met in their current lives. If I didn't believe in reincarnation, of course all this would present obvious contradictions.

Causes and Conditions

My conviction also comes from examining cause and condition, cause and effect. When we look at reality, we can see that things don't happen at random. There is always a reason, always a cause, and always a set of conditions. There are causes and conditions for birth, for death, for sickness or health, for happiness, and for joy. There are causes and conditions for my having been raised as an incarnate lama in old Tibet, for being forced to leave my country and eventually coming to America. The Buddha looked in to causes and conditions for the source of all our difficulties and he found it. But he made an interesting distinction between cause and condition. When somebody died suddenly, as in the collapse of a bridge, and the Buddha was asked why that person died, he gave two separate answers. There was an original cause and then there were conditions. The original cause was that the man who had died had been inflicting the same sort of harm to others at some time, whether he had been aware of it or not. The second answer was that certain conditions had made the bridge collapse—a strong current, a broken beam, or a pillar that had been swept away. He called this the condition. From a spiritual point of view, when you look at why people suffer, you will see two different reasons, the original cause and condition.

In our daily life, we encounter undesirable and unwanted circumstances, lots of them, all the time, even when we're not doing anything to provoke them. We have accidents. Whether in the spiritual or material world, we all struggle with that, and try to find a reason why these things are happening to us. We search for an answer with all possible means. We have autopsies done to explain somebody's death. Or if a plane crashes, we try to find out what went wrong, spending a great deal of time and money looking for the black box. We are fascinated by conditions. The original cause is not so much taken into consideration maybe because science has not yet accepted it or given an explanation for it.

In Tibet, we perhaps looked too much at original cause—steeped as we were in a spiritual perspective— and not enough at conditions. Tibetans may have been so busy worrying about their future life as to have set the stage for the Communist Chinese taking over Tibet. The Communists, who may not have been thinking about original causes at all, came marching in.

As an American-Tibetan, I have had a unique opportunity in that I have seen both cultures. The disadvantage of spending all of one's time and resources on analyzing conditions is that you will never get to the original cause, the source of the problem. You may get a temporary answer for how an accident happened, but as long as the original cause is not discovered, you will never be able to totally prevent it from happening again.

Without the original cause, even if conditions are right, things do not materialize. Even soil that is perfectly moist and well-fertilized will not grow flowers without seeds, just as a seed without the proper conditions will not grow flowers. As pragmatic people looking at conditions, we have building codes and safety codes—lots of things to protect us from mishaps. All of this is done in an effort to prevent suffering, and there's no question that we should continue to try to prevent any suffering that is within our means to prevent. But there is a deeper investigation that searches for the original cause of suffering, the original cause of being reborn, getting sick, aging, and dying in life after life, without choice.

Psychology looks for the causes of suffering, but the only material accessible to it is what happens in the course of one life—the conditions. In an attempt to get to the bottom of a problem, we search adolescence, childhood, and sometimes even try to go back into the mother's womb. This can be very helpful, restoring peace of mind, a sense of security, and self-confidence, yet it might not reach to the deepest layer of cause, and at times it may even create further problems.

Looking back twenty or thirty years, or even as few as ten or fifteen, it's hard to remember exactly what we experienced. It's hard to remember what happened yesterday or even in the last hour. The effort to remember results in a lot of guesswork. A vague memory of fear can turn into an object to be investigated. So a bearded father or uncle becomes the focal point for an investigation into the origin of fear. One begins to wonder, "What did he do? Why am I afraid? Did he beat me up? Did he abuse me sexually?" Fragments of memory come to the surface and we may think we have obtained a breakthrough. But there is no way to confirm whether something happened or not. Some people were abused; others weren't. That creates additional suffering for the family in general and particularly between "the bearded man" and the person suffering.

So should we not investigate our problems at all? That's not the answer. Definitely it's good to investigate. Only make the investigation more thorough. Getting to the bottom of things means going beyond what might have happened in childhood. It is necessary to find the original cause.

We put a lot of effort and struggle into accomplishing our goals, but we fulfill only half of them. If we accomplish even as much as that, we consider ourselves lucky.

In reality, the fact that we cannot do even half of what we want to do is a sign of our lack of freedom.

Not only are we not free to achieve our goals, we are also not free from sickness, old age, and death. That is the truth of suffering, which Buddha saw. What causes suffering? Our negative emotional habits create suffering and blocks to freedom. Freedom may be ours but we have not created the necessary conditions to be able to take advantage of it. When Buddha said he had found a way out of suffering, we can take that as his having discovered a way to freedom. What kind of freedom? The freedom to shape our life and lives.

Traditional teachers tell us that each and every one of us has committed every kind of good and bad action in this life or another. Bad actions lead to more suffering and to a lack of freedom, and that's why it's so important for us to correct our negative habits. Good actions lead to freedom and a good life. That is why it's so urgent that we develop ethics, since we are already expert at making mischief. They also tell us we're in this fortunate life because of our great deeds and the fact that we've been patient, generous, and ethical in previous lives. That is a very good reason for us to develop those qualities.

. . .

I'm not here to try to convince you about reincarnation. That's my culture, my system—not yours. I would simply like to ask you to entertain the idea for a moment, to give it the benefit of the doubt and see how it changes your perspective on your life and your death. You may not get a complete confirmation that there is reincarnation, but you won't be able to rule it out, either. No one has been able to prove that it does not take place.

If you give reincarnation the benefit of the doubt, the question of who we are and where we come from becomes: "What happened between our previous life and this one? Or during our previous lives?" The moment we think like that, our perspective changes.

Enlightened masters have found the real source of suffering, the real cause of trouble, the real block that prevents freedom. They stress that negative emotions—anger, attachment, hatred, and jealousy—are the original cause that keeps us trapped in the cycle of life and death. From negative emotions come negative actions, from negative action comes negative karma, and from negative karma come karmic consequences.

The beginning of freedom from this cycle of suffering is through recognizing that we have anger, attachment, hatred, and jealousy. We have to take responsibility for ourselves and for our actions. It's the right thing to do. By looking at negative emotions, we can get rid of denial. When we see that there is a problem, then we can fix it. Otherwise we'll have to pay for our negative actions with our own body and mind, now and in future lives.

This is not a new idea—that there are negative consequences to our negative actions. Many cultures have used fear to control people. Religions have often used the threat of hell as a means of discipline. In old Tibet, even thieves hesitated to kill because they believed they would have to pay the price of suffering with their own skin. But you can't say religions are there only to threaten people into submission.

Take time to analyze how negative emotions might cause suffering and keep us suffering life after life. Think about the possibility for yourself. If you don't think about it, it will be a huge waste, because as human beings we have fantastic minds. The sky is the limit on what we can do. We have the same capabilities as all of the great human beings who have ever lived. The only difference is that they took advantage of their opportunities. So let's think about it and let's change our minds. Let's make the best use of our capability, particularly that of the mind. We can change the course of our journey once and for all.

The earlier masters say that this life is like a crossroad. It can lead in two directions, one of which is to a wonderful enlightened level. Why not make the best use of it? There can be no better time than today.

Hindu-Buddhist mythology tells the tale of a flower known as the *utamwara*, which is supposed to appear only when Buddha is born, to bloom only when Buddha becomes enlightened, and to last only as long as Buddha's teaching lasts. Buddhists say that we are still in an age of the influence of the utamwara. The possibility for each of us to reach our full potential and become completely enlightened still exists. And even if we are unable to accomplish complete enlightenment within one short lifetime, we can continue in the next life and fulfill our goal.

Two

The Mind
Continues

No more right & wrong
yes it's gone gone gone
gone gone away

—ALLEN GINSBERG

Death is like sleep. *Bardo* is like a dream between death and another life. Then we wake up. When we wake up, if we are lucky, we'll be in a beautiful place, a wonderful pure land, or human family. Or we could end up somewhere else, where everything is burning—the ground is on fire, the walls are on fire, the mountains are on fire, the forests are burning, hundreds of burning acres, and we in the middle of it all. It could be. Everything is possible, though nothing is permanent.

The bardo is like a dream. We may think that whatever sufferings we get in a dream are not real; we say, "It was only a dream." But you really go through the pain, very much so. And the joy, too, when you have a good dream. It *is* real. If you dream you have a stomachache, that's also real.

When you wake up from a dream and look back, the dream is gone; it's in the past tense. Whether it felt real or not, it was just a dream, and it's gone, right? The funny thing is that when we die, when we are dead, and we look back on our life, it is just like that dream. Good or bad, whatever happened is gone now. It is just like waking from a dream and looking back. All the tortures, sufferings, joy, all of them—*pffft*—gone. Good and bad both will be like a dream and gone.

Dissolution of the Elements

What does it mean to say, "I am alive"? What does it mean to you? People will give me their name, mention their profession, even say they have a physical body. I have a funny way of looking at it. I always think that when people come to life, it means that they bring their universe and plug into the general universe. I look at life as a union—the union between the physical identity, which is my body, and me, or rather, my mind. If the physical identity is not occupied by a mind, then it doesn't survive. The separation of the physical identity, the body, from the mind is called death.

How does life work? The physical body is given by the genetic material that comes from our parents to ourselves and is then transmitted to our children. It is a borrowed apartment, a rented apartment we happen to be staying in.

The body is made of four elements—earth, water, fire, air. The flesh and bones and nerves are the earth element. All the fluid in your body is the water element. The heat that aids in processes such as digestion is the fire element. Breathing and circulation are the air element. When these four elements are balanced and we don't have any aches or pains, we call ourselves well. When they're off balance, and one element becomes weaker than the others, we feel discomfort or pain in our physical bodies and it may also affect our minds.

Death is separation—disconnecting. At the time of dying, which may last weeks or even months, the first element to go is the earth element. When the earth element weakens, we get a vision or a mirage of water—it is as though we see water though there is no water anywhere. Some people simply feel they are surrounded by water, though they may not see it. A woman once told me that when her grandmother was dying, she complained for weeks that there was water coming into her room, under the bed, everywhere—though there was no water at all. That's the first sign; it means that the earth element is separating from you and so the water element has become very vivid.

When the water element disconnects, then the fire element becomes vivid and you see smoke, as though the air around you is filled with smoke, as though the room is full of people smoking cigarettes or burning incense. One man complained as he was dying that there was a lot of smoke in his room. The doctors said, "Forget it. It's a hallucination." The fire element was taking over.

Then the fire element signs off and the smoke is replaced by sparks, as though you had thrown burning embers in the air. Now that the earth, water, and fire elements are gone, all that's left is the air element. When that goes, what you see is reflected candlelight—as though the candle is somewhere behind you, and its glow is flickering in the darkness. All the external elements are completely disconnected. When the earth element is gone, you cannot move any more. When the water element goes, your lips are dry. When the fire element goes, you start losing heat. When the air element goes, you stop breathing, and your heart stops beating.

Internal Dissolution and the Meditative State

Now the internal system begins to dissolve. By this time the body is dead, but the consciousness may remain because the internal separation has not yet happened. The indestructible drop, the subtle essence obtained from the parents at the moment of conception now begins to separate. As the father's subtle essence separates, you will perceive a moonlike, whitish reflection. Then the white is replaced by a reddish haze, which indicates the mother's subtle essence has separated, too. Then you fall into darkness. The actual darkness comes as a shock because you've lost your external faculties, then your internal ones, and even the indestructible drop. The shock of plunging into darkness is like fainting, like losing consciousness. You're suffocating, and that makes you feel as though you want to get out of your body. That is the death period, and it can be very short or last quite a while. It is a quiet time when those who have the ability can clear the last obstacles to achieving total enlightenment. One can clearly see in this phase that though the person's heart and breathing have stopped, they are still in their body. There is no sign of decomposition and the skin has a normal glow. As soon as the consciousness departs, the skin suddenly turns gray and the features become sunken around the temples, the eyes, and the cheeks. There may also be nasal and other secretions.

My father, who died at the end of the Cultural Revolution in Tibet, remained in that state for fifteen days. My teacher and the senior tutor to His Holiness the Dalai Lama, Ling Rimpoche, remained in it for fourteen days, and the junior tutor to His Holiness, Trijang Rimpoche, for about fifty-two hours.

Death Is a Sensitive Period

Some people like to think that death is wonderful because, after all, it's a natural process. That may be true, but it's not always that beautiful. The time of dying is a very sensitive period. We're dissolving, withdrawing from all our senses, from our fingers, hands, arms, limbs. We are retreating, retreating, retreating, until finally we retreat even from the seed we collected from our parents, into our deepest point. Our sensitivities become extremely heightened now.

I had an experience once in Delhi when somebody, without my knowing it, gave me some bhang. Bhang is hashish. The bhang was inside an Indian sweet, and it was served for breakfast at a businessman's house. A Tibetan doctor was present along with a couple of senior government ministers. The businessman said, "Rimpoche, you have to take this sweet." And I said, "Why?" He said, "It's a blessing, *prasad.*" If you say no to prasad, it's like saying no to God. The two ministers suddenly got up from the table saying, "Oh, yeah, yeah, we'll collect the prasad later," and ran off. I wondered why. The doctor got one, too, but the businessman said, "Don't give him any more—he has to see patients." I wondered why he said this, but just went ahead and ate a few anyway. They were very nice sweets, and I love sweets.

An hour or two later, everything was very bright and I could hear every tiny sound magnified a thousand times. People talking in the next room sounded as though they were talking inside my ear. The sensitivity was so great that if somebody flushed the toilet, it sounded as though the flushing was in my ear.

Just like that, the sensitivity at the dying stage is magnified a thousand times. You're withdrawing, retreating from your physical body, so mental sensitivity increases. There can be tremendous suffering. You may feel as though you've been buried under a landslide, that you're in the middle of a cyclone, or that you're drowning. Consciousness remains present, but so subtle that even emotional habits are not present. Though these habits become latent during death, they have determined your course.

The Bardo

There is no such thing as a dead person, only a dead body. My consciousness, which came from a past life, remains in my present life and will travel through to my future life, without identity, and unless I am a highly developed practitioner, without memory. Identity does not exist without the points of reference of time, label or name, and events. Since identity keeps changing, who I am, or might have been, doesn't matter really.

The moment I am separated from the physical body, what we call "me," the object to which I point my finger is no longer me. It is separated from me; it becomes my dead body. Until that time, my body is most precious to me. I maintain it, look after it, and even a tiny little pain is unbearable.

Consciousness moves out because the body has become unserviceable. Then bardo leads to reincarnation. It is like a transfer, or a station where you catch the next train.

When we die, how do we transit from this life to the bardo and from the bardo to our next reincarnation? What is traveling? What really travels is a very subtle continuation of us, some kind of very subtle mind, a subtle energy like air. We cannot see it physically, cannot catch any shape or light or form, not even energy. It's too subtle to grasp, far more subtle than atoms and neutrons. It cannot be measured for the time being.

What continues has gone beyond positive and negative identification: The dying mind is neutral and is too subtle to be either virtuous or nonvirtuous. That's what leaves the body and, sooner or later, in its next life, it reverses the process of disconnecting that happened in the dying stage. It reverses it, and the consciousness then begins to take on a new form, awareness, and finally an identity, too.

The karma, or pattern of action, you create becomes an imprint, which travels with you. The imprint is like a life-sized image that shrinks and becomes a tiny trace. It is even more subtle than memory and is not visible. It is stored, and surfaces when the conditions are right.

During the bardo, people take on the appearances they will have as mature adults in their next life. But, at this point, they don't have physical bodies. These beings can see each other, but we can't see them, because we have a physical body. That's where the curtain is drawn.

The nature of the bardo is that you are not so restricted in your movements. You still have a body, but it's a mind-body, so there are no limitations of movement. You go wherever your thoughts send you, and it can be a wild ride. Aside from exceptional cases, people can't see or hear you. You have lost the capacity to communicate in the way a human being is used to doing.

Sometimes the *bardowas*, the people in the bardo, think that they are still alive. They don't know they have died. They may see their friends or loved ones crying and screaming, and they might approach to console them. "Hey, don't cry, don't cry. Why are you crying?" But they won't get any response and that might upset them. They may come to sit in their usual place at the dining table, but they may find someone else there. They won't be served any food and will wonder, "What did I do? Why are they all ignoring me?" The bardowa is sensitive, and life in the bardo is fragile. Each one of those little upsets could kill them and push them into another life in the bardo. These are the bardo's sufferings.

Not everybody will have a prolonged bardo. Some have a very short bardo; some will repeat the bardo seven times. The maximum life span of a bardowa is seven days. Each death is called a small death. The maximum time a person can remain in bardo is forty-nine days. After forty-nine days, the bardowa takes rebirth.

This is one possible death. Then there are two others, according to the tradition, that result from positive karma or actions of body and mind: In one you are received by wonderful beings who show you to a pure land. In the other, there may not be anyone to greet you, but you'll feel like a child returning home.

Most of us don't remember what happens between

lives or who we were in another life, but great practitioners do retain some memories of their experiences and have reported them. There are eighteen volumes of return-from-death stories that give detailed accounts of the bardo and of rebirth.

The Possibility of a Bad Rebirth

We can have a bad rebirth. What I have learned in the Buddhist tradition about hell would make your hair stand on end. When I was about eleven or twelve, I attended a teaching given by the senior tutor to the Dalai Lama, Ling Rimpoche, at my monastery in Tibet. I still remember that I was sitting next to a pillar in front of him while he talked about hot hells, cold hells, razor-sharp hells, hells of continuous rebirth. About two thousand people were there. He talked about the hell realms for three days, and I couldn't stop crying. I was crying constantly, day and night. I was soaked in tears from the fear of falling into the lower realms—and from a slightly artificial compassion at the thought of others falling into them.

A teacher of mine said, "Listen, you can cry, but you

don't have to." He told me to think instead about the sufferings of a daikon radish, a nice radish growing in the mud, with beautiful green leaves. Suddenly a mean gardener comes to pull it out. It is sold to the women selling vegetables, and they sell it to a cook. The cook takes the radish home, then throws it in a burlap sack with other daikon radishes and vegetables. He counts the radishes, cuts them into pieces, chops them, cooks them in boiling water, and serves them to you and you eat them, digest them, and shit them out. That's the suffering of a daikon radish. It made me laugh, and that's how I stopped crying over the fear of falling into the hell realms. I also learned it's not preordained. We don't have to go there, and should we land somewhere unpleasant, we won't be there forever. Each reincarnation is made temporary by birth and death—even in the hell realms.

People think that since they're on a spiritual journey, and they are human beings, things could only get better. That's not so according to Buddha. What will make me be reborn as a human being just as I am now? What will make me be reborn as a pig in the slums of Calcutta? My negative or positive karma, created by my habit of mind and action. Who creates my negative karma? I do. Who creates my positive karma? I do. Why do I create negative karma even though I know it will just make me suffer? I can't help it because I'm under the control of my emotional habits. The bare bones of the problem is my habit of anger, attachment, hatred—those negative emotions.

The thing to do is to correct the habit of negative emotions and turn them into positive emotions. If we can do that, every action, every chore, every effort, every movement, and our daily work will become positive in nature. We won't create new negative karma. And if we purify the old karma, we won't suffer its consequences. It is something we can do and the gain is tremendous. I believe this is true for all human beings—Jewish, Christian, Muslim, agnostic, athiest whatever. We should do this right now so that if death appears tomorrow, or one hour from now, we will not be sorry.

Rebirth

Shock can push a person in or out of sanity or balance. Just like that. Shock will push you into life, into uncontrolled existence.

The transition from bardo to the next life is provoked by the force of a powerful emotion that draws a person to the sexual engagement of parents. The bardowa finds perfect, fertile, genetic conditions that can generate life.

Bardowas may travel free of a body, beyond the laws of physics, but they are tossed about by their uncontrolled thoughts. In their travels, they see everything: cats, birds, dogs, horses, men, and women, all the creatures making love, and are pulled toward them. You are caught where the conditions are right for you. You are drawn toward a condition because it appeals to you.

As a bardowa, you have an attachment to either the male or the female—their lovemaking will draw you. Since you don't have a physical identity, you fall into their lovemaking and get caught in it because of jealousy or aversion. The mind of the bardowa flows in and is caught. Unable to escape, the bardowa dies of rage and takes on a new life. If you are drawn toward the female, you are jealous of the male, and you are born as a male; if you are drawn to the male, you are jealous of the female, and you are born as a female.

From the Buddhist point of view, those conditions appeal to you because of your karma. Karma or no karma, you happen to be passing through; the love-making happens to be happening, you happen to be drawn to it, out of attachment or jealousy. You go to it because you want to participate. It can be attachment; it can be profound love. It can be anger or it can be self-esteem or self-determination. The emotions can be right or wrong, good or bad, but they are strong. These powerful emotions cause the transition from bardo to life.

Conception to me is when the mind connects with the genetic conditions to be able to survive and grow. The sperm reaching the egg and a consciousness entering coincides with that. That's the interdependent system—conditions and circumstances create an identity. Sperm and egg are joined together on this physical level, growing with limbs, eyes, nose, brain, chemicals, beauty, functions, liquid, air, energy. It's as though you have moved to a new apartment—it's the same you, in a different setting, but the style remains the same. There are certain characteristics that you carry from life to life, because every individual has a pattern. That pattern is hard to recognize because, though your style of living and functioning may be the same, you look different; you're in a new apartment and a new life.

Impermanence

We all have this idea: "I won't die today." Everyone thinks like that including people on their deathbed. We visit someone at the hospital. We all know they are dying. They know it, too, but still they talk about what they'll do next week. It's important to remember that. Why is it important? Our troubles come unexpectedly, particularly death. You go see a doctor, and the doctor says, "You're fine." You get into your car, then you have a crash and die. It can happen.

This is to remind people that this life is wonderful, but there are limitations. Before those limitations take over, achieve what you want to achieve. Do something while you are able to. Right now everything is wonderful, happy, beautiful, enjoyable, but that well-being is temporary. It could change any minute. Anything can go wrong at any moment.

This talk of death or impermanence is not meant to make you afraid. The whole purpose of it is for you to have compassion for yourself. And travel well.

Three

ANGER AND
PATIENCE

Colored Bulbs

I once received a telephone call from Allen Ginsberg, who was visiting William Burroughs at the time. Burroughs was worried that his addiction to drugs was going to be a problem at the time of death. My reply was that it was a physical addiction, not a mental addiction like anger. Your anger will bother you much more in your future life and at the time of death than any physical problem. The mind goes with you; the body stays.

When you look at your mind, what do you see? You probably see nothing. The mind itself is not tangible. It has no shape, no color. It is in reality like a crystal-clear lamp shade, and by nature, it is pure. When we encounter that natural mind, it is a good, relaxed feeling.

But mental faculties—such as anger, attachment, faith, love, and so on—change things. They pop up in our mind, suddenly, with or without reason. If you get irritated, anger pops up, and the moment it does, it's as though the clear bulb under the lamp shade had been changed to a red one. The lamp shade now looks like a red lamp shade. If you remove the red bulb and put a blue one in, the lamp shade will turn blue. But if you look more closely, you'll see that the color is coming from the bulb. That is exactly what happens to the mind under the influence of emotions. When a mental faculty such as anger pops up, suddenly the clean, clear mind becomes red or blue or green. The clarity is gone, and our transparent mind has now become a disturbed mind.

Positive mental faculties can also pop up. Their effect on the mind is to make it become more pure, more clean, more sincere, and they can become a habit. Changing our lightbulbs to positive ones means making an effort. We need the will or intention to do so. It's like swimming against the current. It's a struggle. But take action; go against the current, because the effort will pay off.

Human Kindness

There is kindness in every human being. Even if we behave badly at times, by our very nature we are beautiful human beings. It's important to acknowledge that all of us have that nature. And if that beautiful nature were able to function within society, imagine what a wonderful society we would have—kind, loving, and caring. But at the moment we don't function that way: Everybody wants to win. I would like to win over you. You would like to win over me. In each and every life, in the street and in our homes, with all the nations, races, even religions, everywhere, we have this problem.

If our beautiful human nature were functioning, there would be no room for strife. Why is there struggle, then? Because at this moment that nature is only a seed. It can be completely overcome by our negative emotions, particularly fear. So instead of love and compassion shining out, anger, hatred, or jealousy is expressed. Or if there is some kind of love, the clinging, sticky part shows up rather than pure love. Our beautiful human nature is obscured by the temporary obstacles that come up.

Fortunately, our problems are impermanent. If they were permanent, we would be stuck with them. We could do nothing. But our problems, our negative emotions, are like clouds. Clouds float across the sky; they're not part of the sky. Clouds can be removed by the wind, then the sun can shine again. Negative emotions function like dark clouds in stormy weather, but, like the sun, moon, and stars, the kindness and compassion of an individual can shine again in a beautiful open space. Emotions can change; they change within us every minute. We can see within ourselves that we're angry one minute, and a couple of minutes later the anger has faded. But we don't have to sit and wait for the wind to blow the clouds away. We can whistle for the wind to remove our obstacles.

The problems that we face today—the emotional problems, anxieties, fears of being lonely—are the result of nothing but delusion. So we have to work with delusions. We have to work with them in order to overcome them. It is important to remember that you can't make a deal with delusions. If you do it would be like making a deal with the devil—you would lose.

The Cost of Anger

> *There is no error greater than hatred,*
> *And nothing mightier than patience.*

So I strive in every way
To learn patience.

—BUDDHA

Anger is the mind that wishes to harm and hurt. Patience is the mind that holds back from harming or hurting. Anger is most difficult to deal with; patience is most difficult to develop. Patience is the only thing that defeats anger.

Some say that anger is not that bad, that it's fine to get angry sometimes to get the pain off your chest. Some therapists even recommend getting angry. I cannot quarrel with that since I'm not a therapist. Anger, jealousy, and pride push people to achieve goals, at school, at work, and in every other field of life. Though it may fulfill a desire, whatever success is obtained by such means comes at a great cost. The ends should not and cannot justify the means, and that's an important point to remember. A burst of anger will not bring any lasting benefit, though it may result in short-term relief.

Anger is expensive, extremely expensive. It is more than just the fee you pay to a therapist. Spiritually it costs you a tremendous amount of virtue. In everyday life, it costs you a clean and clear, lucid mind. Peace of mind is like a clean, clear, tempting glass of water. A minute of anger is like putting a little dirt in it. Anger makes you miserable and makes everyone who deals with you miserable—your family, your friends, your colleagues, and your society all are made miserable by your anger.

Let's say you had a good night's sleep. You get up. You're happy, relaxed, well-rested, in a good mood. You're looking forward to the day. Then you go out and encounter one little irritation. Maybe somebody blocked your car in and you can't find the person to move it. You get upset. You say, "I'm going to be late. I'm going to be this; I'm going to be that. It's so cold" or whatever it is. And when you get upset, look at your mind. The happy mood is gone. Your face is longer. In a moment, the anger is gone, but it took your good mood with it. You don't get a happy feeling so often. It only comes once in a blue moon and now it's gone.

Anger actually deprives you of having experiences of joy in the body and peace in the mind. And as long as you have hatred, your anger will burn and torment you. No new happiness can grow in you, and whatever happiness you had before will be taken away. You will not be able to rest, at any hour of the day; you won't even be able to focus. You won't be able to concentrate or think. You'll feel as though someone had shot an arrow through your heart. If the mind is disturbed, it can even cost you your health.

How does anger affect our future life? Traditional teachings will tell you that like fire, anger consumes a lot of fuel. Fuel is created by positive virtues. Imagine, in one moment of anger, eons' worth of positive virtue is destroyed. How difficult it is for us to create positive karma. It takes a lot of effort, a lot of thinking, a lot of sacrifice. Then, suddenly, one little moment of anger can destroy all that.

Anger Is Addictive

Anger pops up effortlessly, like toast out of a toaster. It's a habit. We may think we don't like getting angry but deep down we must be getting a certain amount of pleasure from doing so. Anger gives us a temporary sense of satisfaction: "I got it off my chest. I gave her a piece of my mind." Though later we may regret yelling, the regret isn't strong enough to hook us. It's the satisfaction that's hooking us. This is very difficult to see. Most of us deny it. If satisfaction weren't part of it, we wouldn't get hooked to the point where if we don't get angry, we become restless. We are compelled to do it again and again. It becomes very seductive.

And when you let anger go unchecked, it comes much more often. You become irritated, lose your temper, and before you know it, anger becomes a habit. Yelling, screaming, shouting, and tantrums become a habit. You may feel that you have gained the upper hand, especially when the people around you don't fight back. They may be keeping quiet because they don't think it's worth it to argue, because they don't like to scream and shout, or because of social etiquette or a sense of dignity. Whatever the reason, it's not because they're weak and you're strong. If anger gives you a sense of power, you're blinded by rage.

I'm Not Angry, But . . .

There was a man driving down a highway listening to the radio. Suddenly there was an announcement: "On such and such a highway, a man is driving in the wrong direction. Use extreme caution." He looked around and said: "Only *one* person driving in the wrong direction? There are hundreds of them going in the wrong direction!"

How are we going to find freedom? We have to recognize the negative emotions that hold us prisoner. We do recognize anger, we do recognize jealousy, we do recognize them, but we do not recognize—point the finger at yourself—that it is *my* anger, we do not recognize *my* jealousy, we do not recognize *my* ignorance. We like to deny them. I like to deny that I am angry, I like to deny that I am jealous, I like to deny that I am ignorant. If I keep on denying it, how can I recognize it?

Some people think: "Well, anger is bad; I should not show it." And so instead of helping the anger get out, they suppress it. Instead of getting rid of it, they store it up. You have to acknowledge that it's there. A few people, the honest ones, will tell you, "I am angry." Most people say, "I'm not angry, *but* . . ." Right? And many tell you, "I don't have a problem, *but* . . . somebody else has a problem."

You have a problem as large as an elephant inside, however much you may deny it. By denying, you can build up your anger a little bit more. And you can manipulate a few other people in between, create a little more trouble and a little more negative karma. That's what we do. Instead of that, try to acknowledge. Acknowledge. If you can acknowledge that you're angry and give yourself a minute or two to watch your own mind, you will feel a little bit embarrassed, a little soft, a little bit sheepish, too. And when that happens, the power of anger has been cut tremendously.

It may take a week or a month to acknowledge, even a year. Some of us are angry with our mothers and get angry at her all the time. We keep that up for years. But it doesn't matter how long you've been angry, acknowledge it. Then the next time, your anger won't last as long. It will get weaker and weaker, and there'll come a time when you might be able to acknowledge that you are angry while it's happening. Then you may be able to acknowledge the anger coming on even before you actually get angry, and eventually to avoid it altogether.

Tantrums

In the 1960s, when I was head of the Tibetan Language Program Division at the All India Radio station, there was a director there whom I respected tremendously. One day, he had a fit while I was in his office. He started yelling and screaming and hit the ceiling. I started to giggle. I couldn't help it. To me, his face looked just like a monkey's ass, complete with a moustache. He chased me out of his office. That was the end of my respect for him.

When you get angry and hit the ceiling, think, "How do I look?" You really have to think about that. You have to remember, when you lose your temper, when you have a tantrum, when you are controlled by anger, that you look just like a monkey's ass. You are not going to look sweet, kind, nice, handsome, or pretty. You will look like a monkey's ass, and people will lose respect for you.

A temper tantrum to me is a watered-down version of hatred or anger. It's a kind of anger, but not the worst kind, the kind that wishes harm. A temper tantrum is just hot air flying. We experience it as a hot flash in the body. It makes us lose our judgment a little bit, which is why it's not good. A temper tantrum could come from compassion: Your love for your children, for your students, or for your elderly parents might make you scream at them. But if you do it too often, it can easily turn into terrible anger. So don't make a habit of it. You're playing with fire.

The Many Faces of Anger

Anger takes different forms. It sneaks up on us. First comes impatience, then irritation, a tantrum, anger, and finally hatred. There is anger that seethes, anger that freezes, anger that shakes you, and anger that bursts into rage. And then there is anger at ourselves—what we call self-hatred.

Self-hatred takes time to develop. It doesn't just pop up. At first, it's a dissatisfaction. Often it starts because someone planted the idea in our minds at an early age or because some desire was not fulfilled—whatever that desire may be, involving pleasure or money or a goal, however unrealistic. We work ourselves as hard as we can to fulfill that demand or reach that goal. People take two jobs, three jobs, do all kinds of things. They work more, eat and sleep less, there's no rest for body or mind, all because of a desire we impose on ourselves. We often aren't even sure where it came from or why we're pursuing it.

When we work hard and still cannot fulfill our dreams, we begin to develop a dislike for ourselves. We see nothing but faults. We view the fact that we could not fulfill our desires as a failure. Then we say, "That's me, a failure." The unfulfilled desire becomes stronger, and the sense of failure becomes stronger, so we see outrselves as incapable. We don't like to see ourselves as a failure, so the dislike becomes stronger until it turns into anger. The anger grows until it becomes hatred. We actually begin harming ourselves.

If you are angry at yourself, that anger can surface as a dissatisfaction with life in general. Then some people begin to latch onto the spiritual to justify their sense of failure. You tell yourself you don't care about material success. But deep down, anger and self-hatred make you think you're spiritually well off even though you're not. You say that material things aren't important when the reality is you failed at material life and don't want to admit it. So you act as though you don't need anything, pretend to be happy about things, and pretend to be a saint. That is another typical face of anger that people don't recognize. It will only trap you further into negativity. It will give you an excuse to drop out of life, provide a cocoon to hide in instead of facing your problems.

"Never mind" plays the same trick. When you are talking to someone and hit a sensitive subject, they try to hide if you get too close to home. They get upset,

they don't want to show their anger, or they don't realize they're angry, so they say "never mind," and try to
avoid talking about it. Whether you realize it or not, it's
a symptom of anger.

Some people hide the rough edge of anger: They
put on a smooth face, maybe even showing a caring and
loving face, hiding their real feelings any way they can so
as not to think they are giving another person pain. But
really it's a kind of violence. For example: "I didn't lose
my temper. I kept my cool, and he got angry. The more
I stayed cool, the more he got angry." Then they take
pleasure in the fact that the other person is getting an-
grier. That's a case of strong anger, only wearing a another face.

Repression may not look like anger, because you
can't see the desire to harm so easily, but it may harm
the individual more because it's hiding in storage. When
you repress anger, you hold back and don't explode, but
you internalize your anger. You eat or you don't eat. You
start taking out your frustration on anyone—a clerk in a
store, a cashier at the gas station—instead of the person
you're really angry at. Sometimes repression can take
the form of self-affirmation. You may think, "Okay, I'm
going to work hard, teach him a lesson, and be the most

famous person in the world." That is also anger. It may look positive but, from a karmic point of view, it might not be.

A lot of traditions encourage repression but it can create many problems. It only buys time, delaying wrong action. It may in fact contribute to building anger, and make for even greater repercussions. Rebellion is often the result of repression.

Wrongs Are Not Permanent

Part of the reason we get stuck in self-hatred is because we think, when we've done something wrong, that we've ruined everything permanently for ourselves. But nothing is permanent and nobody is irretrievably bad. Nobody.

There is a story about this. In the Buddha's lifetime, Angulimala was told by a guru, "If you can kill a thousand people in one week, you will be liberated and become famous." Angulimala set about stabbing and killing every person in sight. As soon as he had killed them, he cut their fingers off, threaded them on a string, and wore them. That is why he was called Angulimala, "garland of fingers." When he had killed nine hundred ninety-nine people, he was desperate for one more. He looked around but the only person there was his mother, whom he wanted to spare if possible. Then another man appeared, who turned out to be Buddha. He was walking away, so Angulimala said to him, "Come back, I need you." Buddha said, "I'm right here." But whenever Angulimala tried to approach him, Buddha would be just beyond his reach. Finally they got to talking, and Angulimala told Buddha that he needed to kill one more person and then he would be liberated. Buddha explained to him that this was not at all the way to do it, but that he would show him how to purify all his deeds. Angulimala became one of the Buddha's greatest disciples and almost reached total enlightenment.

People are always saying, "Well, I'm no good, I'm terrible, I'll blow it, I'm too young, I'm too old, I'm too sick, I'm too high, I'm too low, I'm too black, I'm too white, I'm too this, and I'm too that."

We have many excuses for putting ourselves down or for feeling like victims. When I was a kid, I was badly beaten by my manager, by my attendant, by my teacher, because that's how kids, especially young lamas, were disciplined in old Tibet. It was not right, but it was what people did. I used to get all kinds of bruises. Sometimes when I rode a horse, I had to stand in the stirrups. If I went to my parents and tried to complain, do you know what they told me? "Qualities come at the tip of a whip." My last beating might have been at the age of seventeen. But I never thought those people abused me, and I don't think I carry the scars of that today. I certainly never thought I was a bad person or unworthy because they beat me.

Don't put yourself down because something bad has happened. The bottom line is that the life the Buddha had is the same life that you and I have today. There is no difference in capability or body or mind. Only effort makes the difference.

Blame

Once I was waiting for a friend to drive me to the airport. He was late, but I didn't do anything about it—like finding someone else to drive me there—because the truth is I was quite comfortable where I was. I missed my plane, of course, and took pleasure in blaming him, though, had I really been in the mood to go, there were a dozen ways I could have done so.

No matter what problem we may have, we like to blame somebody else for it. We never blame ourselves. We say, "I'm right, but she did this and this." We always blame the other. That is our habitual pattern because we are too proud to admit our faults. Our pride makes us not want to look inside. Everybody thinks, "I'm right." Well, not quite everybody. But we rarely think, "I'm wrong," either. Whenever there is a mistake, it has to be somebody else's. If not she, it's the cat; if not the cat, it's the neighbor; if not the neighbor, it's the etceteras. There's nothing wrong with looking in and seeing yourself a little bit.

So it is our own arrogance and our own problem of not seeing, not looking inside, that creates most of our difficulties. No one is free of blame. Everyone has their share, and there is nothing wrong with that. If we had no faults, we would all be enlightened. But we are not. So the problem of anger is natural. There is nothing to be embarrassed about.

If I stress the need to recognize, I am not trying to insult you. I'm not trying to tell you that you're angry, only trying to bring awareness, to get you to acknowledge your faults a little bit. It is not so bad sometimes to put your finger on your own nose. Instead of seeing everybody's faults everywhere, it is good to turn your eyes inward and watch yourself a little bit.

Patience Is the Antidote

Buddha said that patience is the antidote to anger. Patience as I understand it and patience as it's normally understood might be slightly different. In our usual understanding of the word, patience can mean that you don't get upset, that you can wait things out. If people make a mistake, or insult you, you don't mind. You can do very hard work constantly, continuously, without complaining. This kind of endurance is a good quality in an individual, but it will not necessarily produce positive karma or cut anger.

When Buddha said that patience is the antidote to anger, he meant the kind of patience that creates positive karma. That patience involves holding back from hurting and harming, and pushing yourself to care for yourself and others. It is the mind that doesn't get disturbed when others are trying to harm you, or when you are suffering. Patience is not weak. It is full of enthusiasm. It's totally engaged, focused, and concentrated, not a dead-tired donkey climbing uphill under a heavy load.

Patience can help you face difficulties in your life and in your work. The words we usually hear—"I'm burned out," "I can't take it anymore," "I have no energy"—are clear indications of a lack of patience. "Burnout" happens from a lack of patience. If you're working very long hours under extreme conditions and you get tired and need a rest, that is normal. But if you get burned out under normal circumstances, or cannot stand putting in slightly more than the usual amount of effort, then that is burnout from a lack of patience.

When you lose interest and are forced to continue working though you don't enjoy it, you get burned out. You feel, "I can't stand it anymore; I'm out of here; I'm quitting tomorrow; I want a divorce." You are ready to abandon your children, your elderly parents, your job, your friends—you name it. Patience plus enthusiasm creates an interest in life and in work. You'll get tired, but you won't get the emotional symptoms of burnout. The joy you receive from patience and enthusiasm feels a lot better than the tiredness you get when you are burned out: The joy is more powerful, positive, and effective. When you have that joy, you'll notice that you're not getting angry as often, anger won't last as long, and pretty soon it might not bother you at all.

Negative emotions can't simply be overcome by not giving in to them. It takes a number of methods applied together. Enthusiasm happens to be one of them. To cut something tough, you need a sharp knife. Enthusiasm will give your knife its edge.

This kind of patience has nothing to do with becoming everyone's doormat. Some people think, "I am here to accept all the blame and everybody else is right except me—I'm wrong. Or, even if I'm right, I'll let it go." If you do that, people will often dump on you. You may acknowledge fault without having to blame yourself. As soon as you begin to blame yourself, you can become a doormat. Everyone will run you over—with a car, a bike, a truck, a bulldozer. This is not patience, but the loss of self-esteem.

To be self-destructive is not part of spiritual practice. Spiritual practice exists to help oneself, to build oneself, not to destroy oneself. Buddha's aim was to show us that we can build ourselves so much that we can reach total enlightenment. To destroy or undermine ourselves is not spiritual practice. When something goes wrong and you're at fault, blame negative emotions and their source. Don't be angry at yourself.

Patience Protects

A Tibetan monk, a chanting master from the Dalai Lama's personal monastery, on being released from a Communist Chinese prison in the late 1980s, told His Holiness, "There was danger." The monk was not referring to the danger to his life but to the danger that he would submit to anger or hatred. To me, that is a very powerful message.

When somebody literally "tries to get you," what can you do? There is no question that you have to protect yourself. But you don't do that by getting angry or hating the person. There's an interesting example Ram Dass told me once. He was teaching psychology at Harvard University in the early 1960s, a time when many, including him, were experimenting with LSD. Having taken acid one time, he miscalculated and found he was still tripping the day he was supposed to go and see his family for Rosh Hashanah, the Jewish New Year. Ram Dass, whose name was then still Richard Alpert, belonged to a prominent Jewish family from Boston. He shaved, got dressed, and drove over to his parents' house. He said he saw the steering wheel of his car as a coiled snake, but he made it to the dinner anyway.

He was seated across the table from a conservative businessman who did not approve of Ram Dass's way of life. The businessman started criticizing him, and suddenly Ram Dass saw little arrows coming out of the businessman's mouth and heading straight for him, one after another.

Instead of letting the arrows hit him, Ram Dass caught each one and gently laid them on his plate. Throughout the dinner, he caught and lined up every arrow that came his way on the side of his plate. If he had let the arrows pierce him, he might have responded to the insults, but since he was able to divert them, no harm was done.

That doesn't mean that you should think, "I'm going to let anybody do whatever they want to and just be patient about it." If you allow others to harm you, that is not patience. That is pulling the carpet from under your own feet. If someone is doing something harmful and there is no reasoning with them, then the time has come to protect yourself. Even so, there is no need to hate the person. You don't have to do anything against them, but you do have to do something to protect yourself, and if possible, without hurting anyone in the process. You do sometimes have to stop people if necessary. That does not mean that you lose your patience.

Thanks to my teachers, to the training they transmitted to me, my struggle with anger has been much simpler than it might have been. For instance, when I left Tibet, under Communist gunfire, I lost my parents, my family, my wealth, estates, and comfort, my life at the monastery, everything.

Anger didn't overwhelm me. But I did notice a little hitch later on. I didn't have a problem with the Chinese in general, but in 1998 on my first trip to China, I discovered that I had a problem with Mao. When I changed my money to Chinese yuan, I saw Mao's picture on every single bill. The thought of putting his face in my pocket gave me the creeps. It was a strange feeling. Under the circumstances, I had no alternative but to put the money in my pocket and forget about Mao. In order not to be bothered ever again by the idea of Mao's image in my pocket, I took refuge in patience. Patience here means exactly this: not submitting to hatred.

From Anger to Patience

If patience comes easily to you, wonderful. If not, how do you go from anger to patience? When negative emotions are strong, they tend to overpower you: You could never take suggestions, never be able to apply an antidote. You need time. First, find out if you're willing to see whether your anger is valid or not. If you are not willing to do that, then the suggestion is to take a break. Walk outside. Go to a nice place where there's a beautiful view. Divert your attention through something neutral, like nature. When a thought of anger or even violence pops up very strongly and you divert your attention to a neutral level, the force that was pushing you to do the wrong thing is weakened. Once it has been weakened, there's the opportunity to do something else. In Tibet, many of my teachers liked to go up on a high mountain overlooking the valley, to enjoy the fresh air and the view of the valley, the river, and the mountains. They let their disturbing thoughts fly away—if they had them at all—and took in the fresh air. Certain traditions even recommend that you watch the sunset from a slightly high vantage point, standing lightly, bouncing gently on the balls of your feet. Breathe softly three, nine, or twenty-one times, using the out breath as a vehicle to carry your thoughts away. Let your heavy thoughts go with the setting sun and bid them good-bye.

Give yourself ample time to dwell in the feeling of the nice, cool breeze at the top of the mountain, overlooking an entire valley, lake, or river. Stay long enough so that any disturbing impulse cools, not physically but mentally; only don't catch cold.

Who Is the Enemy?

If someone is harming me, I'm mostly going to develop hatred. If they're hurting me, my first impulse will be to want to hurt them back or wish them to be hurt. These enemies become huge in our minds. They keep us from eating and sleeping and from having any peace in our lives.

So, who are they and why are they doing this to me?

Who am I angry at? Where is my anger focused? It is focused on that person, because that person is hurting me, and that person is the source of all my trouble. But is that really true?

I should look to see whether that person is hurting me so as to teach me a lesson and to make sure I suffer. If that is so, did he hurt me on purpose and of his own free will, or did he do so out of fear for himself?

Maybe his intention was not so much to hurt me, as to protect himself. He may not have had a choice. And if it was anger, does he really have free will? He may have thought he wanted to hurt me, but really his own negative emotions are so powerful, so strong, that he was totally misled by misinformation and misunderstanding. How many times have we been overcome by rage, yelled at someone, only to find we had totally misunderstood the situation? Anger keeps us from hearing properly.

We never really know what motivates someone else. When you were a child and your father got angry with you, he may not have wanted to hurt you. He may just have wanted you to learn better or may have wanted to protect you. Maybe your mother forced him to it.

Maybe your sister forced him to it. Maybe your brother forced him to it. Maybe he was conditioned to treat you harshly. Maybe his parents treated him badly and he didn't know any other way. It doesn't mean that harming you was right. Whatever the case may be, we have to find out what conditions may have forced his hand. If these conditions didn't exist, maybe there wouldn't be that anger in him, that act of meanness by him, because there would be no conditions. This is always true. So if it's due to conditions, then almost certainly your father felt forced to do it. He didn't have freedom within himself because conditions forced him. If you look carefully, your father was like a slave to his own delusions. And if he didn't have his own free will or free choice, and he was forced to behave in a certain way, I don't think it would be right to be angry with him at all.

Identifying the Source of Suffering

If a crazy person is behaving like a crazy person, hitting you and screaming at you, there's no valid reason to get angry at that person. A crazy person is crazy. And the one who tries to challenge a crazy person is definitely crazy. You can't get angry at a crazy person, because he or she is overwhelmed by delusions and is not acting out of choice.

If I burn my finger in a fire and get angry at fire, it would be silly because fire's nature is to be hot and to burn. So what I do naturally is to avoid putting my finger, or hand, in the fire rather than getting angry at fire itself.

If a certain behavior temporarily comes up, it's not worth my getting angry over it. It is just a symptom. If somebody lit a huge fire that made a lot of smoke, you can't get angry at the smoke coming into your room. It's not worth getting upset over the symptom. It's easier to open your windows and doors to let the smoke out, instead of getting angry at the smoke.

First, identify the real source creating suffering and obstacles to joy. If you look carefully, you'll find the real enemy, the one who's stealing your freedom and joy and creating your suffering. What do we do when we find the real internal enemy? Should we get angry at that enemy? You can get angry at yourself and destroy yourself, but why not do something about the delusion instead?

Taking Advantage of Difficulties

Tibetans considered the camel a sign of horrifying times in a degenerate age, so they expelled all camels from Tibet. The Mongolians were happy to have them because they could use them in the desert. Likewise, sometimes in our life we encounter what look like difficulties and obstacles. Rather than worrying about them or rejecting them, we can accept and make the best use of them to neutralize the negative, to actually change our negative responses into positive ones.

The Tibetan saint Milarepa is a case in point. At the instigation of his mother, he killed his greedy aunt and uncle and all those who had gathered for a family wedding, by using his powers of black magic to make a building collapse. Regretting his deed, he sought out the great master Marpa, who took him on as a servant and subjected him to very harsh training, which included making him build a succession of uninhabitable towers—round, square, triangular. No sooner had Milarepa built one, than Marpa would have him take it down and build another. Milarepa endured this for over a decade. He not only accepted his predicament, but took advantage of it as an opportunity for contemplation, to accumulate merit and be purified. When he finally received instruction and meditated, he became one of the great spiritual pioneers of Tibet.

My father always used to say, "Whenever any kind of suffering comes, even a tremendous amount of suffering, it is our karma. If we don't pay for our own karma, who will?" Nobody else created it, so nobody else can suffer its consequences. The only hope for happiness, not just for individuals but for a country and the world as a whole, is to abolish our negative karma.

Difficulties will come no matter what we do. A spiritual practitioner can make use of those difficulties. You can turn any kind of mental, physical, financial, or emotional difficulty into a benefit. Joy and suffering are very much a matter of mental perception. Do you know what to do when suffering comes? If you can think, "This is my bad karma, and I hope and pray this suffering will clear it." If you can think like that, it might be cleared.

Wherever it may come from, whenever we have suffering, it is important to protect ourselves from pain as best we can, but we cannot challenge and fight what is unavoidable. Causes and conditions, which may at this

moment be outside of our control, bring it on. The resistance against unchangeable suffering can cause
greater suffering. Instead of not accepting it, let it come.
It's natural. Don't worry about it or fight it, and don't let
it make you unhappy. That will reduce your suffering.

Patience is not a strategy for overcoming your enemies. You may never be able to overcome your enemies.
It is a matter of overcoming the shortcomings of your
mind. If you look at it from a spiritual angle and you are
trying to overcome anger, small pains can substitute for
huge amounts of pain that we're bound to have anyway.
There are a tremendous number of stories Buddha told
on this subject. For example, even the headache of one
morning can substitute for taking rebirth in the hell
realm for a long period.

Whether or not you can do this depends on what
kind of motivation you have. You can see paying taxes as
either a great hardship or an act of generosity. If you see
your money going toward social services and you're
happy to contribute to the welfare of others, then this
thought makes tax-paying an act of generosity that creates positive karma. Everything depends on motivation—not on what you give, but how you give it. It's not

what you suffer; it's how you deal with suffering that can make a big difference.

Seventh-century Indian pundits said, "You can look carefully at suffering itself to see whether it can be corrected or not. If it can be corrected, put all your effort into correcting it. If there's nothing to be done about it, why be unhappy? The unhappiness only adds more suffering to the suffering."

Accept suffering if you have to, but don't suffer unnecessarily or foolishly. There are people who like to get sick and would be happy to be even sicker because they think it will purify them. They don't treat the illness. They would rather endure the suffering because they believe it to be a part of purification. Some people feel guilty if they have made a little money and think they should get rid of it. These are misunderstandings: We need to take care of ourselves, not only spiritually and mentally, but also physically and financially. Yes, when pain is there, we can use it. But I don't think we need any additional pain. We have more than enough.

This particular life provides the fundamental opportunity for freeing ourselves, once and for all, of negative emotions, of uncontrolled rebirth. It is such a waste if we don't appreciate it, care for it, and use it properly. The opportunity may not easily recur or come as often as we think. It is precious. So it's important to make the best use of human life, take the best care of it, and develop as best we can. That is spiritual practice, and if you don't care for it, you are destroying the fundamental basis for any improvement, whether physical, emotional, or spiritual.

We can make a difference to the quality of our lives. We can achieve anything, whether scientific, material, or spiritual, if we are willing to make the effort. So why submit to the same old pattern?

An End to Anger

When you have been entertaining negative emotions such as anger, unless and until you acknowledge that you are controlled by these negative emotions, you continue to give negative emotions room for further growth. But as soon as you begin to see that your actions have been mean, terrible, that it's not the everyday you, then you suspect that it's not you doing it, that it's negative emotions pushing you to it. So check. The way you check is to ask yourself, "Is this my normal behavior or is it unusual? If it's unusual, then why am I doing it? Because I'm angry, hurt, and I want to make trouble for the other person." This confirms that it's your anger, not you. Then it's time for you to take charge. And once you confirm that this is the negative emotion of anger, then it is your job, your duty, and your responsibility to yourself to decide that you will not let yourself fall under the control of any one of those negative emotions. And resolve, "I must free myself from the clutches of this terrible emotion called anger. I pray that I may be protected from anger. I reject anger, help me to reject it, and bless me to end all anger and its root and causes, once and for all."

Bite off what you can chew. When you resolve on Friday that you will not entertain Dr. Frankenstein till Monday, yet you find yourself yearning for him on Saturday, then you pray. Visualize that light and liquid come from the enlightened beings, filling your body completely, washing away all negativities in general and, in particular, hatred, anger, and even irritation. Tell yourself that it is all completely washed away and your body has become of pure light nature and your mind is happy, open, and wise. This visualization was recommended by the great masters and spiritual practitioners who have used it for thousands of years to help themselves and others defeat anger.

Realize What You Have Accomplished

Don't be disappointed if you can't apply patience right away. Even after years of practice, you may find that you're still losing your temper. It's all right. But you will also notice that the power of anger has weakened, that it doesn't last as long, and does not as easily turn into hatred.

Looking back and evaluating is important. Your own achievement is one of your best inspirations. When you realize you have achieved something, it is one of your most reliable sources of strength.

Four

ATTACHMENT AND PURE LOVE

The way attachment functions within the individual is very different from anger. Anger possesses you. It's hot, you feel it, and you can see it coming. Attachment is cool, soft. It's like dipping paper in oil. When the paper touches the oil, though you barely dip a corner of it, a large amount of oil is quickly absorbed. And it's extremely hard to wash out. Likewise, attachment is pervasive. It comes unexpectedly, takes over our entire body, mind, and even speech. Without our realizing it, attachment has taken over. That is the difference between anger and attachment. Anger is rough, attachment comes in gently. By the time we realize it, we are already up to our neck in it.

In the 1700s, in the Amdo area of Tibet, there was an old monk who was very attached to the butter used in Tibetan butter tea. He liked to collect it to reuse it. That recycled butter is called *zhah*.

He fell ill, but he still managed to go to the monastery every day for the morning gathering when butter tea was served. Soon he could no longer carry his cup, so he put a ladle in a bag and hung the bag around his neck. When he could no longer walk by himself, he had two young monks hold him up so he could go and collect his butter. He was so ill, everyone wondered why he hadn't already died.

A famous spiritual master of the time, who was called Gungtang Jampelyang, heard the story and, since he happened to know the monk, decided to go and see him.

"How are you feeling?" Gungtang Jampelyang asked the old monk.

"Well, I am sick," he replied, "but I haven't missed a single morning meeting—I like the tea so much."

"Oh, that's good!" said Gungtang Jampelyang. "And did you collect a lot of zhah?"

The monk said, "Yes! I have collected a lot of zhah."

Then Gungtang Jampelyang said, "You know, I've heard that in the Pure Land of Tushita, the butter is far better than ours, and they give you much more of it, too."

The monk said, "Are you quite sure?"

Gungtang Jampelyang said, "Yes, my teachers told me so."

The old monk said, "Well, since it comes from you it

must be true," and he died two days later, very peace-
fully.

Love or Attachment?

Attachment is an emotional pattern. You see something,
you like it very much, become possessive of it, and don't
want to be separated from it. The feeling is so strong
that your mind becomes completely fixated on the object. You want to own it, to make it yours and yours
alone. You can't think of anything else, you can't do anything else, and you can't do without it. You are fixated.

The English word "attachment" may not give you
the full sense of what I'm trying to convey here—
attachment as a very acute desire, aimed at one thing, an
obsession. You identify with the object of attachment, as
though your sense of self entirely depended on that one
person, job, relationship. The thought of being separated
from the object of attachment can even make you feel
a physical pain in the heart.

Certain kinds of love really are wonderful, beautiful,
and great. Other kinds of love are miserable, extremely

miserable. You have to look into your own mind and try to separate the good from the bad: What is the beautiful part of love, and what is the miserable part of love? In general, we can say that pure love is great, that it is universal love, kindness, compassion. If your love is pure, you want the other person to be happy. You want their life to change and improve, whether you're part of it or not, according to what's best for them as opposed to what might be best for you. Wow. That's great, and really freeing. But we also have tainted love, the love that feels, "It has to be mine and mine only. If I don't get it, I will make sure no one else does!" That is the miserable part of love.

Attachment makes you feel great, even though it is not great. It makes you feel pleasure, even though it is not really pleasure because it doesn't last and it brings other side effects. When attachment is getting its way, sometimes we feel we have achieved, we have conquered, but within a very short period things may change, and what we thought we had starts to slip away. We have not achieved; we have not conquered. On the contrary, we are losing, and we have been defeated. Then the pain is much greater than the pleasure ever was.

Between attachment and love there is a very, very

subtle difference. The line between them is thin and hard to see. Love comes with attachment; attachment comes with love. With every love we have, somehow, one way or another, attachment creeps in. You can tell yourself so easily that you're wishing the best, when you're really wishing for control. And that is why, no matter how hard we try, love is a little difficult. But you don't have to feel bad that your love might be mixed with attachment. Attachment is hard to handle. It is the glue that keeps us stuck in the cycle of life and death.

One way to know whether what you have is attachment is by looking at how something affects you. How does it make you feel, how does it make you behave, and does it disturb your peace of mind?

At first, attachment may bring some excitement and happiness. But within that happiness, within that excitement, if we look very carefully, we will see the heavy demands of desire, a desire that justifies a sense of ownership and belonging. I become very possessive. Then I want it to be exactly as I want it to be rather than the way it is. I want it to be mine and mine alone and nobody else's.

Of course, at the first gentle level of attachment, there will be no rough edges at all. When possessiveness begins, that's where the roughness comes in. Attachment will bring jealousy and anger. All our buttons get pushed, all the lights will go on: blue, red, yellow, all of them. It's like a tiger roused from sleep by a monkey's antics. Further irritated by the noise of the crowd nearby, it roars and then attacks. That will be the end of your nice peace of mind.

The Glue of Attachment

One day, you're out window-shopping and you see something you want to buy, but don't. You go home, think about it, remember how beautiful it was, how you'd never seen anything like it, and you realize you really want it. But by the time you go back to the store, it's gone. You feel the loss terribly; it's like a torture. When that happens, look for the feeling of loss that tortures you—you keep thinking about who manufactures that item and where you might buy one. You don't rest until you find out.

The same thing happens when someone leaves you.

Two weeks later, you find you're just not letting it go. The symptoms are that you feel useless, hopeless; you think you're bad, ugly, uneducated. You begin losing your self-esteem. That feeling may get mixed in with anger and hatred, but you can't let it go. Any news of your former lover excites you, makes you push to find out more.

Attachment also makes you dull. You can't think straight. Your mind is occupied, overpowered. You can think only about what you lost, not about what you might have gained. You think about the pleasure you have enjoyed and mope about the loss. You don't remember the pain you went through trying to hold on to the relationship.

When you see yourself behaving this way, you begin to realize how attached you really are. The realization comes only after checking. If you're checking regularly, there will be no surprises. But we are not in the habit of checking.

In the mid-1970s in Delhi, there was a homeless Tibetan man who needed three hundred rupees for an injection. He went around the hostel to collect the sum, but he died before he was able to get the treatment. After his death, his belongings were disposed of. His dirty old pillow was about to be thrown out when the rustling of paper was heard: thirty-thousand rupees were found stashed inside it.

Attachment to money can become so severe that you won't want to spend any of it on yourself, and you may even completely overlook the needs of someone near you.

I have a strong attachment to sugar and sweets, which probably contributed to my diabetes. When I first came to America, I would eat four or five slices of apple pie a day with two or three scoops of ice cream and chocolate sprinkled on them. Not one—never one—but two or three. When I was a kid in Tibet, people gave me rock candy because they knew I liked it. My attendants at the monastery would take the sweets away, so I hid them between my books. I chewed the candy every night and would fall asleep with it in my mouth. We didn't have bed sheets but woolen blankets made of long yak hair, so all the hairs of my blanket would be stuck to my face the next morning when I woke up.

Addictions are hard to give up because of attachment. People don't like to feel hatred, fear, or jealousy, but they can't help themselves on account of attach-ment. People are accustomed to thinking that it is a noble human sentiment: You love someone or some-thing and you grow attached to that person or that thing. Which is not necessarily so bad, but attachment doesn't stop there—it makes you hate those who dislike you and be jealous of those you love. The world be-comes divided into "for me" and "against me." It is a mis-erable way to live.

Again, Recognize

An analysis of attachment works just like the machine that checks blood sugar levels. You rely on symptoms—thirst, yawning, laziness—but you're never sure until you check your sugar level. Often, you are wrong. Though you think it's okay, it could be high or low. Confirmation is very important. Without it, you'll just get worse.

If you want to shoot an arrow and you don't see the target, it is blind shooting. The arrow may hit anything, anywhere. If you want to be effective, you need to rec-ognize the object at which you are going to aim. When we try to overcome attachment—as with anger or any negative emotion—point number one is to recognize that we are attached. You have to recognize the delusions first and then you can work with them. Ask yourself: What is attachment? What does it do? What is its effect on me? What kind of suffering or pleasure does it give me?

As soon as we start looking for our faults, we find a way to squirm out of them. We say, "I've got it right. I don't have attachment; what I feel is pure love." Or, "My situation is special. My attachment is a special attachment." Everybody thinks that way, and everybody talks that way. Everybody fools everybody, including themselves, just like that.

Then we may even say, "Hey, it doesn't matter, attachment is a delusion, so I can let go of it." That is pretending to have overcome attachment. That is cheating yourself, no one else. Many play that game: "I am over and beyond attachment. My love is pure love." If you do that, you're cheating yourself.

You can go on cheating yourself for a time, but then your life will be gone and you will have lost the opportunity to do something about it. You have the opportunity now, you have what you need, you have friends—everything. If you don't do it now, when will you?

See Beyond the Skin

I saw a beautiful *damaru*, a small ritual drum that was made of ivory at Tibet House in Delhi that I wanted to buy very badly. I didn't have the 700 rupees they were asking for it, and I wanted to take it on credit. But Daisy, my wife at the time, was running Tibet House and said, "Rimpoche buys everything and has no money," so I couldn't buy the damaru. Two decades later, I saw the same damaru in a Tibetan shop in New York for $700, which is about forty-six times the price it was in India. I remembered the drum so well. But after twenty years, it didn't make a nice sound because it had been damaged by moisture. The skin was coming off the drum heads. Nobody else would buy it because of the condition, but still the seller would not reduce the price because he noticed that I liked it a lot. I bought it anyway because of my old attachment to it.

There's no limit to the exaggeration of qualities attachment can project onto a person or an object.

Usually, we carry a preconceived idea of what we want. When someone meets about seventy percent of our preconceptions, we begin falling in love with them. Our attachment adds up the rest. We can think that an ordinary-looking person is beautiful or that someone we've developed hatred for is ugly.

Traditional Buddhist teachings prescribe a strange meditation for attachment. For example, if you have a strong attachment to someone's appearance, looking deeper into the body—into what it consists of, what it's made of, what it is a collection of—will help you see your attachment. Look at the body's processes. Look past the skin, at the muscles, veins, organs. If you can look at the total reality of a body and still be attracted to the person, it might not be attachment but pure love. Pure love is free of the projection of one's personal ideas.

If you find you are attached, you can use it as an opportunity to develop pure love. Instead of clinging, look into the other person's situation. Try to see that their life is just like yours—you both suffer. Take the opportunity to wish joy and happiness to the person. You can think about protecting that person from suffering. Wish the other person all the possible happiness and success, including enlightenment and total freedom. When you feel the pull of attachment, use that pull as a medium for giving love, pure love, cutting desire and projections, cutting exaggeration. Use that pull to purely accept the person as he or she is. And wish them all the best. Don't think, "I wish you all the best," and stop there. Wish them the best and bring yourself closer to them. By making a commitment to giving them love and to helping them, we can turn attachment into love.

Don't Let Your Car Drive You

Not every desire is bad. The desire to eat food, the desire to obtain enlightenment, the desire to be happy and enjoy life, the desire to help other beings. Are these desires bad? Can't be. However, if you do not check with yourself, normal desire can turn into an addiction.

None of this means that I cannot or should not appreciate beauty or beautiful things. They bring pleasure and comfort in life. A gentleman in Hong Kong once said to me, "You are telling me not to have attachment to nice things. What do I do with my Rolls-Royce?" I told him, "As long as you are having the pleasure of driving the Rolls-Royce, that is fine. But, if the Rolls-Royce drives you, then you are in trouble."

Examine an object to which you are attached. For instance, right now I'm looking at my ritual bell. It is quite ancient. The metal has a beautiful, shiny, worn quality. It makes a wonderful, unique sound. I think about its quality, age, and perfect size. These are the things that increase my attachment to it. In order to undermine their hold on me, I have to remember impermanence: The bell could lose its sound. It could crack. Its color could change. Somebody could drop it and break it. Anything could go wrong. Thinking about impermanence cuts down on my attachment.

Recognizing Attachment

If I am so attached to something that I'm willing to sacrifice anything and everything for it, I should observe these thoughts carefully. Is my only purpose to satisfy my desires? If that is so, any action based on these thoughts will create pain and may hurt people, including myself. Then I know that what I am feeling is not pure love but desire and attachment. I acknowledge that

I have an attachment, though I'm not yet able to give it up. If I see that I'm willing to hurt myself and others by my actions, that confirms I am strongly influenced by attachment. I must carefully observe the consequences of attachment, and I resolve right now, right here, that I will no longer submit to it.

Attachment is the glue that will keep me stuck, suffering continuously in the cycle of life without free choice, without freedom. I reject attachment once and for all. I pray to the enlightened beings, light and liquid comes from them and fills me, purifies all my negativity in general and in particular attachment. My body becomes of light nature. I become pure and free of attachment.

Five

EGO AND
COMPASSION

The true enemy is inside. The maker of trouble, the source of all our suffering, the destroyer of our joy, and the destroyer of our virtue is inside. It is Ego. I call it, "I, the most precious one."

"I, the most precious one" does not serve any purpose. It only makes tremendous, unreasonable, impossible demands. Ego wants to be the best and has no consideration for anyone else. Things work fine as long as "I, the most precious one's" wishes are being fulfilled. But when they're not, and Ego turns on the self, it becomes self-hatred. That self-hatred will eventually burn the house down.

First, Ego separates me from the rest of the world and sees "I" and "me" as the most important. Then "I" becomes "my," as in *my* friend, *my* enemy. I love my friend. I hate my enemy. I help my friend. I harm my enemy. That's where attachment and hatred begin. They don't come out of the blue.

Then the concept of "my" gathers strength. "My" becomes important to me. An ordinary cup, when it becomes *my* cup, is worth more. So, too, are *my* body, *my* country, *my* religion, or *my* sect.

I am the most important, and to protect myself, I need to get my share. You are out to get your own share at my expense, and I am out to get my share before you can get it. We are facing each other, perceiving each other as separate. But if *you* were not there, *I* couldn't be here. So here and there, this side and that, me and you, self and others, all of them depend on each other. Here is based on there; there is based on here. They depend on each other.

"Who am I," in a way, is Ego's question. We say, "I am Nawang Gehlek," "I am American," "I am a lawyer," "I am a mother," "I am outgoing," but those are just labels and they change. Identity is not permanent; it doesn't exist the way we think it does. It is based on certain points of reference—a name, a time, and a physical shape—and those change all the time, even if you don't believe in reincarnation. The "I" is not fixed. It's not permanent. We are young, then old; we are fat or thin at different times; we are sick or well. We are married or single. Our names change. If identity were fixed, we would become a totally different person with each change.

Nawang Gehlek exists because Gehlek's body exists and is the base of identity, and then there is a mind to go with the name and the body. The name Gehlek is the label of that identity, the road sign pointing to it, and a reliable mind has to acknowledge that combination of elements to say that Gehlek exists. That is the conventional "I," and we need it to function in everyday life. But my ego thinks it doesn't depend on any of them; it thinks that I exist by myself. That's a wrong perception.

Ego sees everything as independent. Ego thinks a table exists by itself because it's a solid wooden table. Somebody gave it to me. It's mine. I paid for it, so it's my table. Actually the table exists interdependently: It stands on the ground, it is made of wood and the molecules within the wood, and it has a top and four legs. If one leg were missing, it would be a broken table. If the legs were cut off, it would be a large tray. If a molecule were missing, there would be no wood. The table would fly into pieces. Ego doesn't know that.

And then, if you search for Ego, where is that "I, the most precious one," "I, the dictator"? You won't be able to find it. People might say: "Well, of course I'm here. I exist." But where? Where does the queen bee permanently reside? Is it one with the body? Or separate from the body? One with the mind? Or separate from the mind? Is it my identity? Or separate from my identity? Is my body me, or is my mind me? If my body is me, then which part? My blood? My heart? My ribs? My brain? And if my mind is me, which part of my mind is it? My thoughts? My emotions? My perceptions? My senses? You can take the whole body apart, but you won't find any one point where you can say, "This is me." You can take the whole mind apart, and you still won't find it. That is the absolute truth. That doesn't mean you don't exist. That doesn't mean you don't have thoughts, feelings, and perceptions. That doesn't mean that you don't have relationships or that you don't form judgments, because there is a relative truth, too. You do exist: That is the "I" that gets you through everyday life. But "I, the dictator" is another thing altogether, a thing we don't need at all.

Human beings have a natural instinct for permanence, and the ego sees "me" as independent. It sees a table as independent. It wants to experience everything as unchanging. We don't need Einstein to tell us it isn't so. Because we're born, we die. Because something comes into being, it will disintegrate and change form. Light changes to dark, night to day, and subatomic particles dance in empty space and cannot be measured or fixed in either time or space. Einstein's equation $e=mc^2$ proves that matter and energy are conserved. When an atomic bomb is detonated, matter and energy are converted into each other but not destroyed. One thing is left out of this equation, though. The universe is not made of just matter and energy; it is made of matter, energy, and consciousness. Consciousness cannot become non-consciousness. It cannot be obliterated. It changes form, but it continues. Matter, energy, and consciousness, time and space are all part of a moving, changing, breathing, totally dependent enterprise. Nothing is as solid as it seems.

I always say that if the Communist Chinese had not taken over my country, I would never have come to America; and if I hadn't come to America, I wouldn't be living and teaching here. That Tibetans have lost their country is tragic. If everything is relative, then it depends from which side you look at it. The Chinese may have a different opinion.

It is exactly like Russian dolls: You keep opening them, hoping to find the last one. Science has been searching for the last particle, the irreducible one. The atom was it for a while, but then we found electrons, protons, neutrons, even quarks. Stephen Hawking believes that a last doll exists and that one day it will be found, but I was taught to think that no matter how many dolls you open, there will always be a smaller one inside, and a smaller one inside that one. If we did find the last particle, then we would be living in a static and permanent universe. Nothing would ever move or change.

According to Einstein's theory of relativity, there is no fixed, objective reality, and any measurement depends on the point of view of the person who is measuring and the speed at which they are moving. Are they traveling toward or away from the object they're measuring? Or at an angle? All of these questions have a bearing on any conclusions one draws, since there is no fixed point of reference.

If there is no fixed point of reference, then who am I? Who is it, pretending to be that solid "me"? You've certainly heard stories about rulers with a second in command who becomes so powerful that the ruler becomes helpless, useless. The Ego and I have that type of relationship. Ego rules completely. It's less than me, but it controls me completely.

"I, the most precious one" is an impostor pretending to be me. It feels solid, and it thinks it is in control, but actually it's just a collection of thoughts, of ideas, and of fears. How do I know it's not the real me? My interests and those of Ego are different. I want peace and happiness, but mischief keeps being created. Deep down, I don't really wish to hurt others, but somehow, I keep doing it. I don't really want others to fail, but when they succeed, jealousy takes hold of me. Deep down, we each have a good and wonderful nature that has the potential to become as wise and loving as Buddha. We are made of the same stuff as the great masters, and the same stuff as Buddhas. But my ego is in terror of losing its life and wants to protect itself at all costs. If you get too close to seeing it for what it is, Ego will project its fear of being annihilated. It will reaffirm itself with anger and attachment to make itself more solid. Like a queen bee, it uses all the bees to fulfill its commands, no matter what the consequences might be—and those bees are jealousy, pride, and anger. Otherwise "I, the most precious one" might be destroyed, though I, the person, would survive and go on to a better life.

Finding the enemy and kicking it out is not that easy. It's harder than dealing with anger or attachment because we think the Ego is us. How do you spot it? Wait for someone to insult you. Wait for your pride to be hurt. Wait until someone accuses you of something you didn't do. "I, the most precious one" will immediately get angry at the one insulting you; it will turn that person into an enemy, and then, afraid the other person was right, will turn the anger onto itself. It will make you depressed, make you think you are a loser, make you think you are the worst person who ever lived.

I had many opportunities to experience this. The first came when I was about fifteen years old, during one of my examinations. Out of 10,000 monks at Drepung monastery, only about a dozen took this examination each year. It lasted an entire year and took place in different phases. At one point, I had to go around to different fraternities within the monastery to be examined. At these debates, anyone could ask you any question they wanted in front of hundreds of other monks and teachers.

I was originally supposed to go to a fraternity where a lot of my classmates and learned seniors would be. The class leader told me jokingly, "When you come to my fraternity, I'll make sure you never even open your mouth." I was afraid of going there so I canceled and chose a fraternity that had only two outstanding members, who I was sure would not show up. One was a teacher of mine who was about to become the abbot of my college. The other was a very learned *geshe*, or scholar.

As the debate started, I noticed that an extra cushion with a brocade cover was put on the floor, and I thought, "Uh-oh—the teacher is coming." Whenever anyone got up to ask a question, my teacher would immediately take over the debate and the person asking the question just stood by. After a while, the geshe also showed up. He, too, started asking questions. For each one, I drew a total blank. He would debate around the subject and make it clear to me, but as soon as I showed I understood what he was talking about, he would go on to another topic. He asked me eleven questions, and every single one was at first a total blank to me. It was extremely humiliating.

I cried so much that night and thought, "I know nothing." Until then I had such pride; I thought I was so clear on every topic. I decided, "There is no point in my studying any more. I'll go to Southern Tibet and become a solitary meditator." My mind was made up. My attendants threatened me: "Where are you going, stupid?" And they gave me a couple of slaps. I didn't hit back, but I didn't listen, either. I don't think I slept that night. A little after sunrise I started to leave, and going down the steps of my house, I encountered my teacher. He gave me a long lecture on how great the night before had been. He said, "What great understanding you have! But you can't expect to be Buddha, to know everything—you're not Buddha yet." It convinced me to stay and finish my examination.

Did you ever ask yourself where your desires come from, why you work so hard to achieve, why you're so sensitive to others' criticism, why, when you get what you worked so hard for, it doesn't really satisfy you?

It all begins as the desire to protect yourself, as self-love that turns into a monster and a taskmaster dictating your every move, supposedly in your own best interest, to secure for you the most money, the best position, job, life. It tells you that you have to be better than your neighbor, brothers, sisters, parents. It tells you, when someone else gets lucky, that they are taking your share. It orders you to work hard to satisfy its desires, even if it means sacrificing your health. It tells you that you are the best, the smartest, the most capable, and that you should make sure everybody knows it. It tells you that you should push away and destroy anyone who disagrees with this plan. It tells you to grab anyone who agrees with it and hold them tight.

Who is telling you this? Ego, not you.

In order for a spark to catch, there has to be flammable material. That flammable material is Ego. It catches fire when it's protecting itself. The flames that burn are anger and obsession, pride and jealousy. The fuel that keeps the fire burning is fear.

If a friend says something and I lose my temper, is it my friend who has caused my anger? No, my friend is part of a series of conditions that has led me to snap. And if I can't let go of a relationship that's ended, is it the person who left me who created the obsession? No, that person was part of a series of conditions to which I reacted. If the cause were outside us, everyone would react the same way to everything. So your boss is not responsible for your hurt pride; your parents did not create your rage. We blame conditions, while the problem—and the cause of our problem—is inside.

Magic

In Tibet, a lama of my rank was accorded several privileges, such as a large retinue. The monasteries and villages would receive such a person with incense burning, trumpets blowing, banners waving, yellow umbrellas flying, thrones put up. When I left Tibet, it all disappeared practically overnight. To find myself in such a situation, where I hardly had food or a place to sleep, hurt my pride. I was not invited to stay in the best cottages but shuffled around to makeshift barns and bamboo huts. Among my peers, those who had been able to bring quite a lot of wealth from Tibet tried to establish themselves as bigger and higher-ranking than they were, while those higher in rank than I, and more learned, were in even worse conditions than I was. They, too, had been reduced to specks of dust. I kept this emotional struggle to myself, but sometimes it made me cry with the sadness of loss and sometimes it made me laugh.

Though we were the same people, the same society, our circumstances had changed. It was a great lesson for me—realizing that title, family, background, wealth, everything is truly like a magician's creation or a star in the sky. When the magic goes, the creation goes, too, just as, when the sun rises, stars go from the sky. It was truly dream-like and painful, but it taught me that I should adapt to any condition, anywhere.

My struggle did not last very long. One day, I heard that the former abbot of Loseling, the college I had belonged to in my monastery, had returned from the Indian plains because he was not well and had been sent to the hospital in Bomdila, where it was cooler. I went to visit him in his room, and when he got up to greet me and I saw his outfit, I burst out laughing, just could not help it, which is very bad protocol. He was wearing a woman's skirt and a man's pajama top. Neither he nor I knew that it was a man's pajama top, but I did know it was a woman's skirt because I had seen some in *Life* magazine when I was still in Tibet. He spun around before me, saying, "When you go down to the plains, this is what they give you to wear, whether you are an abbot, an incarnate lama, a learned geshe, a monk, or a layperson; this is it." That probably helped me—it made a big impact on my conscience—that anything can happen, and one should be adaptable.

Five Arguments to Prove the Ego Wrong

Ego experiences itself as being at the center of the universe, and it sees its place there as permanent. How do we challenge this misperception? Argue with Ego. Argue over how it views itself and others.

1. *We all want the same thing.* There are people you love, people you don't like, and people you don't feel one way or the other about. The truth is that each one of those people, regardless of how you feel about them, wants happiness, just as you do. They want to be free of suffering, just as you do. Can you really say anyone deserves to suffer? How can you make a distinction? Everyone wants to be in a good mood, have nice dreams, and be at peace, just as you do. They have unfulfilled desires and, just like you, they deserve to have them fulfilled. Their happiness matters as much as yours does.

2. *How reliable is the label of "friend"? How reliable is the label of "enemy"?* Suppose we're crossing the street and a car is about to hit us. In that instant,

knowing that our life is about to vanish like a dream,
is it worth hanging on to our hatred for someone?
Or our attachment to someone? In the face of death,
our prejudices and old quarrels often become mean-
ingless. The only difference between me and someone about to be hit by a car is that they have a
clearer idea of when they're going to go. I'll be in the
same position as they sooner or later, only I don't
know when. It could be tomorrow, or years from
now. Knowing I'll have to leave everyone and everything behind, is it worth hanging on to my hate or
attachment now?

3. *We rely on the kindness of others.* Everyone,
whether we know them or not, has affected our lives
in some way—whether it's by manufacturing a part
to fix our car or by growing the wheat for the bread
we eat. If you look at it from the perspective of reincarnation, in one form or another we have existed
since beginningless time, so every single living being
at one time or another has been connected to us. All
people have been our nearest and dearest, have put
their lives on the line for us, have even been our
mother, have washed and fed us. They may have in-

sulted and harmed us, too, but they have more often done things to sustain us. And any harm they caused us was probably the result of fear. Today's enemy may have been yesterday's lover. We don't know. It's possible. Let that idea take root in your mind.

If I decide to crush my ego, I couldn't do so without other people: When I try to practice patience, if I keep myself from harming or hurting someone, that person who pricked my anger gave me the opportunity to practice patience. When I try to turn attachment into pure love, the person I am obsessed with gave me the chance to try. I could not survive without the kindness and generosity of others.

4. *We're all in the same situation*. We all suffer equally, and every last one of us who is born will die. If I'm a doctor faced with three dying people, can I really say, "I'll only treat the one I love"? Maybe there's no time to help them all, but the desire to do so equally should be there.

Since I will die and you will die, that means that everything is impermanent. There is no such thing as anyone who can remain a friend forever, or anyone who can remain an enemy forever. We can see that from our own life. A person we vow to love forever turns into our worst enemy in the courtroom. Or, someone we didn't get along with becomes our best friend. Seeing "friend" and "enemy" as solid, unchanging entities is Ego's blindness. But "friend" depends on "enemy" just as east depends on west, night depends on day, up depends on down. What you do affects me, and vice versa. They say that the movement of a butterfly in China affects the course of winds in the United States. Our bodies, our identities, and our lives are completely intertwined. We are not permanent, we do not exist in isolation, and no one is by nature either an enemy or a friend.

5. *Follow the example of enlightened beings.* When you look at great beings like Buddha or Jesus, at prophets and saints, do they make a distinction between people? No. They have no likes or dislikes. They want to help everyone equally. The traditional teachings tell us that the enlightened beings feel about each person as a mother does about her only child. They also say that Buddha feels the same about the person who comes to massage him with sandalwood oil and the one who wants to cut off his arm. Each is equally

dear to him, and he wants to help each of them, because both suffer and want happiness. This may be extreme for us, but it is possible. I saw my masters live their lives in that state of equanimity. No one came to chop off their arm, but I saw them behave with equal compassion toward someone who treated them badly and their closest disciple.

When you see "I, the most precious one" for what it is, that is the beginning of developing wisdom. When you really understand and experience the interdependence of all things, the nature of reality, that is wisdom. But is that enough to achieve the goal of total freedom from suffering? Probably not. The negativity has to be replaced by positivity. Anger has to be replaced by pure patience or understanding. Attachment has to be replaced by pure love. Jealousy needs to be replaced by care, love, and affection. Wisdom alone is not enough. Love and compassion lead to developing the ability to choose a life we want. When we give up Ego, what do we replace it with? We exchange "I, the most precious one" for seeing others as the most precious.

The final blow to "I, the most precious one" is to

begin the work of giving our happiness and taking on the suffering of others. Ego thinks it should have the best, so deliberately giving it the worst knocks it down. This is a visualization practice called *tonglen*—giving and taking.

In the beginning—if you are truly practicing—don't try to visualize so many people; just one will do, perhaps the person you love, your own child, or anyone you are dedicated to. Visualize that person sitting before you; then let out your breath through your right nostril along with all your positive virtuous karma, all your love. Give it all to benefit that person without hesitation. That is the practice of love. Then take in through your left nostril that person's source of suffering—that is the practice of compassion—and let it hit the culprit, Ego, on the head.

At this point there might be some hesitation—I am sure—to take on the suffering of others. If the thought frightens you, then start by taking your own future sufferings, the sufferings you will experience tomorrow, in the weeks to come, the months to come, the years to come, the lives to come. Take them now and dissolve them in your heart into the nature of reality.

We can use this practice to take advantage of our

difficulties instead of letting them upset us. We are experiencing the result of something we laid the seeds for in our past, and we should be happy that soon it will be gone, out of our system, and that we will have survived it. Then we can remember to genuinely pray that a little ailment or fear, or whatever it is, can keep others from having to endure the same or worse. The traditional teachings tell us that by the power of compassion one little suffering can save us from having to suffer something much worse in the future. A small financial difficulty can substitute for a million years as a hungry ghost. A small headache can substitute for a limitless eon in a hell realm. If we can look at it that way: "Yes, I've been in an accident, but I'm alive," or, "I was wounded, but at least nobody made the wound worse," then our problems just won't seem so big.

After a while, draw in the people you really love, the ones you are willing to do anything for—take their sufferings. All the sufferings are in the form of a dark cloud in the heart. Your breath pulls that dark cloud out of them, or out of yourself. At your heart level, Ego is a little candle burning. The dark cloud enters and blows out that flame. *Poof,* it's gone, destroyed. And all those people, since you have sucked out the negative cause of their suffering and the suffering itself, will be free of both. On top of that, you give them your luck, your joy, your bliss, and your wisdom in the form of light. And they are filled up by it, and become very happy.

Six

TRAINING THE
MIND

"Do the Meditation Rock"

Tune: "I Fought the Dharma, and the Dharma Won"

If you want to learn
how to meditate
I'll tell you now
'cause it's never too late
I'll tell you how
'cause I can't wait
it's just that great
that it's never too late
If you are an old
fraud like me
or a lama who lives
in Eternity
The first thing you do
when you meditate
is keep your spine
your backbone straight
Sit yourself down

on a pillow on the ground

or sit in a chair

if the ground isn't there

Do the meditation

Do the meditation

Learn a little Patience and Generosity

Follow your breath out

open your eyes

and sit there steady

& sit there wise

Follow your breath right

outta your nose

follow it out

as far as it goes

Follow your breath

but don't hang on

to the thought of yr death

in old Saigon

Follow your breath

when thought forms rise

whatever you think

it's a big surprise

Do the meditation

Do the meditation
Learn a little Patience and Generosity
Generosity
Generosity
Generosity
& Generosity

All you got to do
is to imitate
you're sitting meditating
and you're never too late
when thoughts catch up
but your breath goes on
forget what you thought
about Uncle Don
Laurel Hardy Uncle Don
Charlie Chaplin Uncle Don
you don't have to drop
your nuclear bomb
If you see a vision come
say Hello Goodbye
play it dumb
with an empty eye
if you want a holocaust

you can recall with your mind

it just went past

with the Western wind

Do the meditation

Do the meditation

Learn a little Patience

& Generosity

If you see Apocalypse

in a long red car

or a flying saucer

sit where you are

If you feel a little bliss

don't worry about that

give your wife a kiss

when your tire goes flat

If you can't think straight

& you don't know who to call

it's never too late

to do nothing at all

Do the meditation

follow your breath

so your body & mind

get together for a rest
Do the meditation
Do the meditation
Learn a little Patience
and Generosity

If you sit for an hour
or a minute every day
you can tell the Superpower
to sit the same way
you can tell the Superpower
to watch and wait
& to stop and meditate
'cause it's never too late
Do the meditation
Do the meditation
Get yourself together
lots of Energy
& Generosity
Generosity
Generosity
& Generosity!

—ALLEN GINSBERG, 1981

Guarding the Mind

If you don't watch your mind, it will be like letting a monkey into a museum without a guard. The monkey will take a big brush and paint over all the paintings. With jealousy he'll paint them green, with anger he'll paint them red, with attachment, blue—he'll put paint all over. So it's time for us to catch that monkey, make it stop, and watch it. You don't want to destroy the monkey—he has a right to be there—but you have to watch it. And if you watch it and train it properly, it can be useful.

Why does the monkey jump around? It looks to us as though it's in the monkey's nature to be mischievous, to create trouble without worrying about the value of the objects he's destroying. But really the monkey just has a bad habit. All he needs is one little signal, and he's off and running: Somebody looks at you funny and your anger immediately rises to the occasion.

When we try to change the monkey's bad habits, the first thing we run into is resistance. Forget about the long-term patterns; even short-term ones we've had only a month or two or, even for a couple of weeks, are difficult to change.

For instance, every day you go to work by a certain route. One day you need to take a different route to pick someone up, and it becomes very complicated. You may say yes to somebody, you'll agree maybe because you can't say no. You say yes, but in your heart of hearts you think, "I have to get up earlier. I don't even know what road to take." But, then if you actually do it, actually get up an hour early, it's not that bad. If you take a different route, it's not that bad, not that difficult. And if you keep watching your mind, sometimes you'll be a little embarrassed, too. You'll catch yourself. And when that happens, it's not so bad. In fact, it's a good sign.

How to Meditate

In reality meditation is nothing but getting your mind used to focusing. Concentrated meditation is focusing to the point of total absorption. How do you get absorbed in it? By getting used to it. By repetition, by practice. Is there any other way? You do it, and do it again, until it becomes familiar, until it becomes part of you.

Allen Ginsberg's poem "Do the Meditation Rock" says most of it. Stay comfortable and alert. Don't slouch, and you'd better not lie down—you might fall asleep.

The head should be leaning slightly forward with the eyes cast down along the line of the nose to an imaginary point five feet or so before you. Your gaze should be relaxed and unfocused. If the eyes are cast too high, mental wandering may result; if too low, depression, or sinking, easily sets in. The shoulders should be held level, the lips together and lightly closed, and the tip of the tongue placed against the palate, behind the top front teeth. This prevents thirst from developing when one engages in prolonged meditation.

Finding an Object

If you use your breathing as an object of concentration, that's fine. But what is recommended here is to take one step beyond the breath and concentrate on an object.

You can concentrate on an object such as a Buddha's form, or an image of Jesus, a Star of David, a religious symbol, or a light form representing the divine. You can take whatever object you want, but something that inspires you will be the most helpful.

Study the image and then visualize it in front of you, at about eyebrow level, one body length away from you. When you visualize the image, clarity and stability will come and go. If you try to bring Buddha's face and nose and eyes into focus then you lose the feet, the legs, the lotus seat he sits on, everything. If you have the feet and legs, then you don't have the head and hands. The first problem we encounter is that. So the idea here is that whatever you get, even if it looks just like a yellow or white lump, keep it. And once you can concentrate, keep the image constant in your mind.

Obstacles

When we try to split wood, we have to hit the right spot with our ax. If you hit the right spot again and again, it will cut the wood in two pieces. If you hit all over the place, you won't cut anything at all. Having a trained mind is like being able to hit the same spot over and over again. You can have total control over where you put your mind. It will focus on whatever subject you place it on. Two hundred things won't come up at the same time.

Negative emotions bring a kind of focus, but the focus is in the wrong direction. When you're angry, or obsessed, all distractions are blocked. The mind will not have any freedom to think differently. Meditation's job is to block the negative emotions from interfering. They don't get entertained. When they come knocking and you don't answer the door, they won't make surprise visits so often. Sometimes you can meditate very clearly, but sometimes you can't; sometimes you are nervous and sometimes you can't think anything and sometimes you can't sit down, not even for five minutes, because you feel tired for no reason.

If you're having trouble, you can do a breathing exercise to settle your mind a little. Using your finger to block your left nostril, breathe in through the right; then block the right nostril and breathe out through the left. Repeat three times, then reverse the process, inhaling from the left and exhaling from the right three times. Then inhale through both nostrils together and exhale together through both nostrils. Three plus three plus three is nine—nine rounds in all.

Feel the air coming in and going out. Visualize the air as a sort of bluish incense smoke. You are creating a diversion, turning the attraction or attention of your mind to something other than the anger, other than the attachment, other than jealousy, or other than whatever. So it provides a bridge from negative thoughts to positive thoughts.

If doing it once doesn't work, you can do it twenty-one times. You can build twenty-one bridges. And if you have all the time in the world, build one hundred bridges. When, through the breathing meditation, you find yourself more at ease and relaxed, then start focusing again.

It is useful to meditate many times a day, but for a short time each session. Don't overdo it. The most important thing is continuity. If you do it one week very intensely, and then take a break for a week or a few months, you won't get any results. If you can do ten minutes a day, after some months, you can begin to feel it, to taste it. The mind has to learn how to watch the mind. Once that happens, you don't have to sit in meditation posture all the time.

Analytical Meditation

Once you are able to stabilize your mind a bit, change what you're focusing on, and turn your mind to subjects. What are the subjects? Exactly what we've been talking about in this book: what a good life we have, how we are going to deal with death, cutting anger and attachment, letting go of Ego, developing love and compassion. The point is to develop a new habit. So you focus, stabilize the mind, and when you feel comfortable, you begin to debate with yourself over these questions. This is called analytical meditation. Use the material in these chapters to help you begin the reasoning process. When you come to the conclusion that you have a great life with tremendous spiritual opportunity, that Ego has been the one stealing your joy, that you can turn anger into patience, attachment into love, that other people are all your nearest and dearest, or whatever you're analyzing, then bring your focus to that point. Concentration will make your conclusions become part of you. That's how you really eradicate negative emotions, through the combination of concentration and analytical meditation.

The Purpose of Meditation

When I was three or four, I was living in a cave with my teacher, Gen Yungtrung. One day he called me outside and said, "Look over there on that rock." A lizard was digesting a scorpion it had just eaten. It was sitting almost totally still in the sun, keeping its belly warm on the rock. Its eyes were open, and it was sucking air. My teacher said, "Look, the lizard is meditating."

The message he was giving me is that, without using the mind, simply sitting with one's mouth open or closed and doing nothing, is not that effective. It might slow you down from your busy life, it might relax you, it might even help you feel better. But that will not serve the purpose of meditation. The purpose is to eliminate negative emotions and fully enjoy positive emotions. Concentrated meditation can reduce the strength of negative emotions a bit, but it can never eradicate them. Therefore, analytical meditation is a must.

So you have to work solidly and build up one realization after another. As realizations build, all kinds of by-products will come up: psychic abilities, channeling, encounters with enlightened beings, visions, and so many other things. Don't pay attention. Just throw them away. They are by-products: nothing to be surprised at, nothing great.

When I was about thirteen, a very strange thing happened. In the monastery, I walked by where the images of the protectors were, and when I passed the female protector, Palden Lhamo, the *mala*, or rosary, I was holding suddenly flew out of my hands, about twenty feet up, and landed on the hands of Palden Lhamo's statue. Everyone around me, all my teachers and attendants, acted as though nothing had happened. It was never discussed, and I completely forgot the incident for some thirty-odd years until a friend of mine, an Austrian monk, asked one of my teachers to compose a long-life prayer for me. In the prayer that Lochö Rimpoche composed, there was a verse describing the incident, and it all came back to me in a flash, especially the fear I had felt. I couldn't even breathe, it was such a terrifying feeling. The mala was made of simple wooden beads held together by string—how could it have jumped out of my hands? Those who were with me saw what happened, and Lochö Rimpoche remembered who they were and told me their names. I am sure that my care-takers and teachers consulted my parents, and that together they decided to encourage me to forget the whole incident, and to treat it as an unwanted distraction so I would concentrate on my studies.

Healing the Mind

At the monastery where I studied in Tibet, each of us attended different teachings, studied many topics, and had to put them together for ourselves, to make a path that we could follow. It was presumed that the teaching was never just based on mental knowledge. In the end, all the teaching, debating, practice, and meditation had one focus: to eliminate negative emotions.

If you are sick and you want to get better, you have to take the medicine prescribed. Just getting a prescription from the doctor and looking at the medicine bottle will not help you. Ultimately, no one holds your hand and takes you around. So it is time for you to watch and to heal the mind, to gain experience and wisdom for yourself. No one can do it for you.

Two Truths

Normally, people think there has to be one truth only.
But in the Buddha's experience, which he shared with
us, we all have two truths and our life is totally based on
them—the absolute truth and the relative truth. The
absolute truth is not measurable. The relative truth is
what allows us to measure, make judgments, take posi-
tions, take sides—your side, my side—all are possible
because of the relative truth. The point of reference of
relative truth is the truth that society accepts. It is the
way we function every day. The point of view of absolute truth is that nothing exists the way it seems to.
Absolute truth holds the mystery of life. You need both
to function.

For those who understand absolute truth, perception changes tremendously. Everything they see—the
walls, the windows, people, the road—is no longer
strong, solid, absolute, intact. What they see has sort of
softened: Even a window is made of all kinds of particles, particularly glass frozen by gas. The particles are
joined together, and if there's the slightest damage to
one of the particles, the whole thing falls apart. Those

who understand interdependence begin to perceive all animate and inanimate objects like that—as particles coming together. The walls, flowers, human beings, they are no longer a solid thing. Perfecting that understanding will lead one beyond the laws of physics.

Whether we recognize it or not, our life is based on both the relative and the absolute. Wisdom is an understanding of that. The path to freedom is wisdom and compassion. Freedom is the result, the perfection of body and mind.

There is an abstract way of understanding, and there is the understanding that comes with experience. Both are necessary. The quality of understanding improves all the time.

You try to achieve the highest possible goal for yourself and others by applying love and compassion and wisdom to your life. Buddhism is very interesting. It can be condensed into a handful and yet the complete path would be contained within that. Or it can be presented with enough detail to fill the universe. Here, I am cutting it down to the bare bones.

Learn a little bit, then think, then meditate and acknowledge whatever conclusions you may have come to. Through that you can heal yourself. Once you're able to remove the mind's obstacles, then your pure nature can definitely shine.

When it does, you not only help yourself, you begin to help others. Then you are no longer in a sorry state; you are really getting to a wonderful state. And I believe that is how you can begin to have a beautifully functioning life.

Seven

A GOOD DEATH

Death is definite, as we know. No one can avoid it. Even spiritually developed people such as Buddha could not avoid it. No one has ever lived forever. No one reading this book will live forever, no matter how old, young, beautiful, rich, poor, or highly developed that person might be. But instead of running away from the thought of death, we have a better chance of doing something for ourselves if we take a look at what's coming or at least try to imagine it. Not only will this help reduce our fear, it will lay the groundwork for us to take advantage of the opportunity to transform the dying process into a process of enlightenment. And if we can't accomplish that, at least we can have a better death.

Whatever life force we have was there from the beginning. There is no extension possible, and the days, weeks, months, and years are drawn from the original supply we were given. One day, it will be like a dry pond after all the water has evaporated. Our conditions for living can easily become causes for dying. The chemicals in our bodies deteriorate. The wrong food or the wrong medicine can have a bad side effect.

We should accept this now. If I wait until I'm actually dying, it will be too late to do anything. So I must accept that I am definitely going to go and that death is definitely going to come for me. Nobody knows when. Since nobody knows when, it could be next week, next month, or next year. I have no certainty that I'll even be here tomorrow or an hour from now. So if I understand this to be so, I must resolve to use whatever time I have to put my anger, attachment, and ego to rest. When I die, when my consciousness leaves my body, what can I take with me other than the karmic imprint of good and bad; virtue or non-virtue; positive or negative? I'll need plenty of positive imprints. In fact, I want only positive ones. But if that's not possible, at least I want to be able to connect with my good fortune before I connect with any negative karma I may have accumulated.

Though death is nothing more than the separation of the body that we have used in one life from the mind that accompanies us into every life, strong emotions are bound to surface at the time of death. Death is the end of all our activities in this life, good and bad. We'll suffer at the thought of not seeing or feeling anything anymore, of not being able to be with or talk to loved ones. Not letting go is our biggest problem. Say what you have to say to the people who matter to you, or write what you have to write. But beyond that, hanging on to resentments or to intense attachment is not good, either for the person dying or for those left behind. It's important to use your understanding and your willpower to cut bad feelings, and if necessary, cut them drastically.

Buddha had a number of extraordinary disciples in his own lifetime, among them one named Maudgalyayana. One of Maudgalyayana's disciples was in the grip of very strong attachment, so Maudgalyayana decided to take two of his disciples on a magical trip. First he showed them a huge mound of bones. One disciple asked, "What is this?" Maudgalyayana said, "These are all the bones from the bodies you had in previous lives." Then Maudgalyayana showed the disciple who suffered from attachment a skeleton with a snake slithering through the eye sockets, the rib cage, up, down, and around every bone. Maudgalyayana told the disciple, "This is you in a previous life. You had such a strong attachment for your body you couldn't let go of it, so you were reborn as a snake that lived in your old skeleton." It's an ancient story, and maybe just another fairy tale, but it gives you a picture of what attachment can do.

How Do We Begin Preparing?

The best thing to do to prepare for death is to practice patience, love, and compassion in your daily life. Practice patience whenever you can so that anger doesn't arise; train yourself in pure love so that attachment doesn't arise; check your ego so that its grip of fear is destroyed; and try as much as possible to develop unconditional love and compassion. If you can do that every day, then you won't panic at the time of death. Positive thoughts will become a habit and will arise naturally. And if you happen to be there when someone else is dying, you can help them by telling them what you know.

Look back on your life and see what was good in it. Don't regret what might have gone wrong. Many things are bound to have gone wrong. We're human beings, and we make mistakes. In spiritual practice we make mistakes all the time; that's why it's called practice. So remember the good things. We have tried to be morally just throughout our lives—which means we tried not to cause any harm, and we tried to keep our commitments. No matter what negativity or negative karma we may have accumulated, it's not permanent. It's changeable. The way it can be made positive is through purification. There is no need to take the negative with you if you have genuine regret, if you've resolved not to do it again, if you have done the sort of meditation that can serve as an antidote, and if you've made some kind of spiritual compensation to those you've hurt.

If you have committed actions that have harmed others or yourself, do not magnify them. If the memory of those actions comes to haunt you, just push it aside. Remember that throughout your life you have tried your best to be a good person, so this is not the time to think about your terrible deeds. Don't let them bother you. You have already taken care of them with purification and other thoughts you are applying, and somehow it will all balance itself out.

Whatever positive karma you have, whatever good you've done, consider it immense. Remember each and every instance of goodness in your life, no matter how tiny, and think of it as immense. This will sustain you, so think about it, remember it. Even if it is negligible, imagine it as infinite.

Don't be afraid. Fear has tortured us throughout our lives. It's just the Ego talking, making up stories. Think that you have seen and understood this clearly. You have crushed the Ego completely. If fear comes over you, remember that it is a false perception. It's Ego's play, and Ego is wrong. Remember to tell yourself that Ego is already gone.

Don't be surprised by what you're going through. Each and every phenomenon is impermanent. So whatever happens while you're dying, remember that it's impermanent and absolutely normal. Remembering all this as you're dying is the way to set the stage for a good transition into your next life.

To do a spiritual practice is to sleep with it, live with it, and die with it. That's how it can make a difference to your life. As long as it remains something distant, something holy up there somewhere, it won't be of any use to you. Negative emotions will stay with you as long as that "something holy" stays up there somewhere, far from where it can do you some good. If you only pray once in a while, how do you expect it to have an effect? Some blessings or rituals may give you a little buzz for a while, but that's about it. And what does that do? Nothing to your negative emotions. To tackle your negative emotions, you have to live, eat, drink, sleep, and die with your practice—that's how it makes a difference.

A Good Death

My friend Allen Ginsberg always used to say, "I don't have proof that there is reincarnation but I must give it the benefit of the doubt, because if there is, and I have to go through it, I should be ready; I don't want to miss the opportunity to help myself." And when his time came, he was ready.

He called me to tell me that he had been diagnosed with a terminal illness and had four months to live. He was surprised at how he took the news. He thought if someone told him he was going to die, he would hit the roof. But he found he was quite prepared to go. He called friends to inform them that he was dying. He started celebrating his life and the fact that it was coming to an end. He sorted out his personal affairs.

Not long after that, he had a stroke, fell into a coma and I went to be with him. His loft was filled with people—many artists, poets, and performers who knew and loved him. I went into the bedroom, I said a little personal prayer for him, then I started the ritual for his dying.

By midnight, he looked as though he was about to go, so I completed the ritual and left. At about 2 A.M., I was told that he woke up, looked around, then closed his eyes and passed away. He remained in his body, in a quiet meditative state, until about 11:30 the following night.

Before you die, make sure the environment where you find yourself is free of disturbances that might create negative emotions. Keep attachment and anger in check. In Allen's case, he wanted and got an open death. Others may want a quiet one. Your environment should be as you want it, and your wishes must take priority over your family's wishes.

Take care of whatever you need to take care of so that you don't worry about what you're leaving behind, so that you can be like a bird sitting on a rock ready to fly, with nothing holding you back. Whatever you decide to give or bequeath, do it while you are still strong and clear. If you can, do it yourself instead of leaving it to an executor. It's also better if you clarify with your children and family where everything goes so there might be fewer difficulties among them after your death. Whatever you're giving, don't give it with any strings attached. Don't let attachment or anger influence your decision. That will haunt you later, as well as create misunderstandings among those you love. It's important to be very generous. It will help ease your attachment.

We have a strong attachment to food, clothing, and fame, or in simpler language, we are attached to people thinking highly of us. It's easy to give up food and possessions, but not our reputation. Even someone meditating in some deserted no-man's-land still hopes that a solitary shepherd minding his sheep will find out about him and tell people in the village.

If there's anything holding you back, get rid of it immediately so it won't be there when you are about to die. It can really interfere with the process.

There's an interesting story about this. One of my masters, Gomo Rimpoche, was a funny person. He did not act like a big incarnate lama. He was married, had a family, and was known mostly as the "father of the children's orphanage home No. 15," in Mussoori. He had a small number of very solid students. Two of them had been officials of the old Tibetan government and left Tibet for India in the mid-1950s. They were very old men in failing health, and they were eager to die while they were still lucid so that they could apply meditation at the time of death. In Tibetan culture, such meditation was something often done among experienced practitioners. With Gomo Rimpoche, they decided the date on which they should go. They made preparations, gave away their belongings, and made arrangements for their house servants.

But when the appointed day came, one of those two officials did not die on schedule. Gomo Rimpoche was at home with his children when somebody came to tell him the first official had died and asked him to please say some prayers. He did, and was expecting a second person to come and tell him that the second official had also died, but nobody appeared. Rimpoche was afraid there had been a problem, so he went to that man's house to find out what had happened. He was told, "Oh, this morning he got sick and had to be taken to the hospital."

Rimpoche went to the American Hospital and found the old man in the Intensive Care Unit. They wouldn't let him in, so he disguised himself as a janitor and sneaked in. He asked his student, "What happened?" The man said, "I started to get all the signs of death, but then all of a sudden they reversed back, and it was so painful. I was screaming and yelling so much that I was taken to the hospital."

The man was a good practitioner and should have been able to transport himself easily to a pure land. Rimpoche could not figure out what might have gone wrong. Then he noticed that his disciple was wearing a brand-new, nice-looking shirt. He asked him, "Where did you get that shirt?"

The old man replied, "It's nice, isn't it? Do you like it? A friend of mine gave it to me the day before yesterday, and I put it on this morning."

Rimpoche said, "I like it very much; please give it to me."

But his student hesitated. "I don't know, I really, really like it."

Rimpoche insisted, "I want that shirt, and if you don't give it to me, we will have nothing more to do with each other."

So, the old man took the shirt off and Rimpoche ripped it up right before his eyes. After that, the official was able to die very easily.

. . .

No matter what happens during the dying process, or what you go through, don't forget to remain in a positive frame of mind of love and compassion. Don't let pain or worry cloud your concentration. If you practice this now, then by the time death comes, you'll be used to it. People who do tonglen all the time, the giving of love and taking of suffering, can die with tonglen on their breath. You may find it hard to take the sufferings of another to flatten the Ego within yourself. It may seem frightening, but that's only because you are not used to the idea of it. In actual fact, you're not taking or giving anything—it's just a way to train the mind to be adaptable to whatever may happen. When you get used to it, you will find that it is good and relaxing and joyful. It will even make you feel happy.

Though you may have taken care of everything, anger and attachment can still arise, particularly anger over dying. People often ask themselves, Why me? Why am I dying when I've lived such a good life? You're dying because it is unavoidable. Remind yourself that death is natural, so nothing unusual is happening. When your mind is calm and quiet and you're resigned to dying, the next step is to influence your mind with positive thoughts. If you believe in God, try to think of God's greatness and die with that. If you are Buddhist, think of Buddha. Or think of your guru, who is inseparable from Buddha. Or think about compassion or love. If that's not possible, with a clear sense of anticipation and excitement, think of a beautiful land where everything is limitless and open and there are beautiful beings waiting to help you. Keep this strongly in mind until you lose consciousness. Visualizing this way can make your future life better.

Learning the Road

During the dying process, many things happen that can seem frightening. Our hearing goes, our eyesight goes, and eventually we'll lose them altogether. Also, our clarity and lucidity will go. That can be very frightening. But it's important to remember that dying is a process everybody goes through. It's absolutely normal.

As the elements of the body dissolve—earth, water,

fire, and air—and the mind begins its process of separation, you may experience sensations of heaviness, of drowning, of a strong wind blowing. And with those symptoms come the internal signs of dissolution. The reason to talk about these signs and symptoms is so that they won't take you by surprise. If you're expecting them, you'll be able to focus on influencing your mind positively. In Tibetan Buddhism, there is a meditation for recognizing these signs and symptoms, which many people do every day so that when they die, they may be more familiar with them. Here's a visualization:

I see water as in a mirage
It's the earth element signing off and I can no longer
* move*
I see smoke as the fluid in my body dries up and I
* can no longer swallow*
I see red sparks in a darkened room like a handful
* of burning embers—*
the source of my heat is dissipating
I see the flickering of reflected candlelight as I stop
* breathing*

I see a whitish color as the subtle essence of my
   father is separated from
the subtle essence of my mother
And a reddish color as the subtle essence of my
   mother also dissolves
I fall into total darkness and leave my body
I see moonlight, crisp, clear light—my own pure
   nature

If you can go through all these stages under the influence of positive thoughts, of your faith, love, and compassion, and with the expectation of pure beings coming to help you, if you can reach the clear light, the cool freshness after the time of darkness, that is a great achievement.

If you can do better than that, then Buddha or God or Jesus or Truth or any of the enlightened beings enter your body from your crown and become one with your mind to lead you through the transition. If you can do better than that, remember the nature of reality, how everything exists in relation to everything else. Add to that the wish that every sentient being should be free from suffering. Know that they may have false perceptions, but that in reality all are pure clear light. Pure being, pure nature is within us. We don't have to search for it outside of ourselves. In absolute reality, everything is pure. Think that it's all pure. "Nature pure. Everything's pure. Naturally pure, that's what I am." Think that.

Not everyone dies slowly. In an accident, there may not be time to notice the signs of death. If you were to die suddenly, try to remember compassion, try to remember that everything is pure, and try to remember your source of inspiration. And don't dwell on attachment or hatred.

If you keep remembering all this often, then you will remember it when the time comes. Do not force yourself to do any particular thing; do whatever suits you best of the options I've mentioned.

Pure Being

When you see the signs of the elements dissolving—water, smoke, red sparks, flickering candlelight—then you know that the body is about to separate from the mind. Soon you'll see a whitish light, then a reddish haze, then darkness. Right at that moment is when you have a chance to work with your pure nature to become enlightened. That's when you can transform your subtle mind, your primordial mind, into an enlightened mind, if you can hold the encounter and if you really know what to look for.

In the dying process, the bright light, which can sometimes create the illusion of a tunnel since it appears after the period of darkness, can also lead us to the primordial mind. The primordial mind is pure and remains pure no matter what. Whether we've had a good life and positive experiences or a bad life filled with negativity, the primordial mind is not influenced or changed by either. It is pure, like a ray of sun. And, when faults such as attachment or hatred arise in us, they are like tarnish on gold that doesn't stick and doesn't change the fundamental nature of the gold. The nature of the primordial mind itself is never affected.

Just as there is an indestructible physical drop that separates when you die, there is also an indestructible continuation of energy and consciousness that carries your imprint of karma. That drop never separates. That mind or consciousness is in an extremely subtle form— it is clear, still, and lucid. That is what travels with us throughout our lives. We can connect with it to transform our minds into enlightened minds and choose our next life. Though this can also be induced through certain meditation practices, death is an opportunity everyone has to encounter the primordial mind.

This may seem like sheer speculation, and maybe it is. But Tibetan Buddhism is a positive tradition: It is based on the notion that we can turn ourselves into completely wise and loving beings. I, personally, have seen the effect of these teachings on many people, both Asian and Western, and my experience tells me it's true. Imagining yourself as a completely wise and loving being, visualizing that you are one, convincing yourself, is part of ultimately attaining that state. It's uncharted territory, so we use these maps to help us make real what we imagine to be possible.

After Death

One evening when I was in my early teens, I was in my monastery room in Drepung. It was twilight, and I was sitting on my bed reciting what I had memorized that day for the resident teacher. Suddenly, my first teacher,

Gen Yungtrung, from the retreat area to which I had been sent to study when I was three, walked in wearing his usual robes. I stood up immediately and the resident teacher also got up saying, "Gen, Gen, are you better?" Gen Yungtrung did not reply. He walked over to the altar and, with folded hands, looked carefully at each image. Then he walked over to me, touched his forehead to mine, and told me something I don't remember. He smiled at the resident teacher then walked out of the room. We called after him, "Please come and sit down." But outside there was no sign of him. We asked some people by the entrance to my quarters, but nobody had seen him.

At the very moment that he came into my room, I later discovered, Gen Yungtrung was dying in Lhasa, six miles away. I guess he had come to say good-bye and to let us know that we would remain connected.

In my tradition, taking refuge is the turning point, the official line you cross when you want to become a Buddhist. Why do we take refuge? We are looking for a source of protection—protection from those things that might cause us to have a difficult time at death and a difficult future life. Buddhist refuge is three-fold: Buddha; Dharma, the teachings; and Sangha, the community of practitioners. We know by now that Buddha Shakyamuni cannot reach down from somewhere and snatch us out of a rough spot or lift us into a heavenly paradise. Only we can help ourselves. So how can we find a source of protection if we are ultimately responsible for ourselves? That source is within us: It is the material we have within us that can be turned into a Buddha, and it is the Dharma within us that is our own spiritual development. That is what helps us live every day and what helps us in life after life. The archaic meaning of "incarn," the root of incarnation, is "to cause to heal." While we live and when we die we have a chance to heal our minds.

One of the last times I saw my father, he said, "When I die, I will not come to you to seek your help. I hope you can achieve the same thing." He was saying that he would know, when his time came, how to depart from this life and enter another. I hope many readers will be able to help themselves as he did. May you and all beings have happiness, be free from suffering, from attachment and hatred, and find the joy that has never known suffering.

Appendix

A Short
Practice

People always ask, "What practice should I do every day?" My answer is, "Keep a watch on anger, attachment, and Ego all day long."

When you wake up in the morning, think the way Allen Ginsberg once told me he did: "I am happy not yet to be a corpse." Be happy to be alive and decide that you want this to be a good day and that you want to be good and kind to everybody. Fit the day between this first thought and your last before falling asleep at night, when you can dedicate whatever good happened to the benefit of yourself and others. You can also regret any harm you may have caused, resolve never to harm again, make some kind of spiritual compensation for it. Then practice meditation as an antidote.

If you want to practice concentrated and analytical meditation, you can start by saying the prayers below.

What do these practices achieve? Refuge renews our source of inspiration; generating unconditional love and compassion sets the proper motivation; the seven-limb prayer helps us to accumulate merit or luck in developing our minds. Mantras protect the mind and keep it on track. But you can leave them out.

You can engage in concentrated and analytical meditation during or after the mantras and before the dedication.

First, invite the enlightened beings. Feel their presence and take refuge, however you do that. If you are Buddhist, you begin by saying *Namo Buddha, Namo Dharma, Namo Sangha* three times. Then, you can say these prayers.

Prayers

REFUGE

I take refuge in the body, speech, and mind of the enlightened beings.

GENERATING LOVE AND COMPASSION

May all beings have happiness,
May they be free from suffering,

May they find the joy that has never known
  suffering,
May they be free from attachment and hatred.

SEVEN LIMBS

  I offer my body, my speech, and my mind
  The best I have to give,
  Both actually arranged here before you and
    imagined
  Multiplied millions of times to fill the space between
    us.
  I regret and vow never to repeat actions that caused
    suffering
  I rejoice in those that caused happiness.
  I request you the enlightened beings
  To remain till I become like you.
  I request your wise and compassionate guidance
  And dedicate any merit to benefit all beings

Mantras

TAYATHA GATE GATE PARAGATE
PARASAMGATE BODHI SOHA
The mantra of true reality, the true nature of existence,
of interdependence. It protects you from disturbing obstacles.

OM MUNI MUNI MAHA [SAKYA]MUNI YE SOHA
This mantra links you to Buddha, who has not only
overcome rough delusions but also selfish interest and
subtle delusions. With this mantra, the body, mind, and
speech of all enlightened beings are linked to our very
body, mind, and speech. *Soha* lays the foundation for
the union: May the qualities of your body, mind, and
speech enter my body, mind, and speech.

OM MANI PADME HUM
This is the mantra of the Buddha of Great Compassion.
Om represents body, mind, and speech. *Mani*, or jewel,

represents method; the method is love-compassion, helping others, being totally dedicated. All of those ideas are represented by the word *mani*. *Padme* is lotus, or the clarity and understanding of wisdom. The mantra links our love and compassion to that of the Buddha of Love and Compassion so that ours may increase until they are of the same nature. And we link our wisdom to that of fully enlightened beings, which is unlimited in clarity and knowledge. We link whatever wisdom we have to theirs, to reach up to their level. *Hum* is the union of wisdom and method.

OM TARE TUTTARE TURE SOHA

This is the mantra of the feminine embodiment of love and compassion, Tara, the mother of all Buddhas. *Tare:* One who has the proper method and the love to lead us out of the suffering of rebirth without choice. With Tare we name her. *Tuttare:* One who protects us from the negative emotions that can destroy our spiritual practice. *Ture:* She who heals all illnesses, both physical and mental. Also if you have any addictions, you can concentrate on her, ask for her help. *Soha* lays the foundation.

Dedication

By this merit
may I quickly attain the state of a perfect being
and take with me
every being without exception.

SUGGESTED READING

His Holiness the Dalai Lama, *Speech of Refined Gold*

Pabongka Rimpoche, *Liberation in the Palm of Your Hand*

Dilgo Khyentse, *Enlightened Courage*

Geshe Rabten, *Treasury of Dharma*

Chogyam Trungpa, *Cutting Through Spiritual Materialism* and *Journey Without Goal*

Shantideva, *Guide to the Bodhisattva's Way of Life*

Lati Rimpoche and Jeffrey Hopkins, *Death, Intermediate State and Rebirth in Tibetan Buddhism*

Gomo Tulku, *Becoming a Child of the Buddhas*

Chang, *The Hundred Thousand Songs of Milarepa*, Volumes 1 and 2

Robert A. F. Thurman, *Life and Teachings of Tsong Khapa* and *Essence of Refined Gold*

ACKNOWLEDGMENTS

I met Allen Ginsberg in the early 1990s and liked him right away. He was a brilliant man, very interested in the possibility of a life beyond the present one and in Buddhist teachings. He seemed to like me for that, and also because I reminded him of his late master, Chogyam Trungpa, who was responsible for introducing Tibetan Buddhism to America and whom I saw a lot of in the years when I was living in Delhi and running Tibet House.

Allen was very kind to me and never missed an opportunity to teach me the background and depth of English and American literature and language. Thanks to him and to Sandy Finkel and Aura Glaser, who brought me to this country, I began to understand the Western way of thinking, and that had a huge impact on me.

Once Allen gave a workshop called "Spontaneous Poetry," and he insisted I come. He asked people, "What are you thinking? Say it now." He asked everybody and I kept my mouth shut. Then he turned to me and said, "Rimpoche, what are you thinking?" I told him what was on my mind. I said, "I don't want to end up in the shoes of Jim and Tammy Faye Bakker." They were spiritual teachers involved in a big scandal at the time. He said, "The way not to fall into that trap is to make sure you keep nothing hidden in any closet. No matter what it is, don't hide it. Keep everything out in the open." I followed his advice, which was really great. Allen himself had an open life and an open death. He's been a source of inspiration to me for his kindness, openness, straightforwardness, authenticity, and caring. He was totally and completely himself, and he showed me how comfortable I could be in my own skin.

He wanted to do a book with me in which he would illustrate what I wrote with a poem. But he died before we could do that, so I have included his poem "Do the Meditation Rock" in the chapter on meditation, to honor that wish.

There are so many people who have helped put this book together that I cannot name them all here. I'd like to thank Gini Alhadeff for lending me her beautiful language; Amy Hertz, not only for editing, but for inspiring me and pushing me—without her this book would never have materialized; and Mark Magill for his skills in organizing the book.

In addition, I'd also like to thank the following people for their kindness, caring, and support: Francesco Clemente, Carole Corcoran, Madonna Gauding, Philip Glass, Kathleen Ivanoff, Kathy Laritz, Chee Eng Lau, Wee Lin Lau, Kimba Levitt, Diana and Jonathan Rose, Brenda Rosen, Colleen Smiley, Marianne Soeters, Nena Thurman, Anne Warren, and Jeanne Zackheim.

About the Author

The grand nephew of the Thirteenth Dalai Lama, Gehlek Rimpoche was born in 1939 in Lhasa, Tibet. At age four, he was recognized as the reincarnation of the abbot of one of Tibet's major monasteries.

As an incarnate lama, Rimpoche received specialized, individual training in Tibetan culture and religion at the nation's largest monastery, Drepung, which at one time housed more than 13,000 monks. Gehlek Rimpoche entered Drepung the year he was recognized. He was taught by some of Tibet's greatest masters.

In 1959, Gehlek Rimpoche was among the thousands of monks and laypeople who fled Tibet, forced into exile by the Communist Chinese who had occupied Tibet since 1951. In India, Rimpoche was among a group of sixteen monks who were chosen to continue specific studies with the great masters, including the

Dalai Lama's personal tutors, who had also escaped Tibet. He attended Cornell University in 1964 on an exchange program. He worked for All India Radio as well as in the Tibetan government-in-exile to help settle refugees and develop schools. He edited and published more than 170 volumes of Buddhist texts from rare manuscripts that would otherwise have been lost; the copies that remained in Tibet were destroyed by the Communist Chinese. At the age of twenty-five, Rimpoche gave up monastic life and chose to serve the lay community of Tibetan Buddhist practitioners.

In the mid-1970s, Gehlek Rimpoche was encouraged by the Dalai Lama's tutors to begin teaching in English. He was a research consultant at Case Western Reserve University, in Ohio, and an instructor of Tibetan language at the University of Michigan, in Ann Arbor. Since then, he has gained a large following throughout the world. In 1988, he founded Jewel Heart, an organization dedicated to the preservation of Tibetan culture and Buddhism. Jewel Heart, based in Ann Arbor, has chapters in Chicago, New York, San Francisco, Cleveland, Lincoln (Nebraska), the Netherlands, Malaysia, and Singapore.

A member of the last generation of lamas to be born

and fully educated in Tibet, Gehlek Rimpoche is particularly distinguished for his knowledge of English, his understanding of contemporary society, and his skill as a teacher of Buddhism for the West. He is now an American citizen.

Transcripts by Gehlek Rimpoche

If you are interested in reading more of Gehlek Rimpoche's work, below is a list of transcripts that are available. They can be purchased through:

Jewel Heart
207 East Washington Street
Ann Arbor, MI 48104
734-994-3385
www.jewelheart.org

Ganden Lha Gyema; The Hundreds of Deities of the Land of Joy
Karma; Actions and Their Consequences
Love and Compassion
Six-session Guru Yoga
Self and Selflessness

Lam Rim Teachings; 1987–1991, 4 volumes

Transforming Negativity into Positive Living

The Three Principles of the Path to Highest Enlightenment
    by Je Tsong Khapa

The Three Principles in a Short Commentary

Healing and Self-Healing Through Tara

Three Main Short Vajrayana Practices

Guru Devotion: How to Integrate the Primordial Mind

Solitary Yamantaka Teachings on the Generation Stage

Odyssey to Freedom

The Perfection of Wisdom Mantra

Lojong, Training of the Mind in Eight Verses

Lojong, Training of the Mind in Seven Points

Shantideva's Guide to the Bodhisattva's Way of Life

Vajrayogini

MARVEL KNIGHTS

BLACK PANTHER

MARVEL KNIGHTS

BLACK PANTHER
THE CLIENT

PRIEST
Story

MARK TEXEIRA &
VINCE EVANS (#5)
Art

JOE QUESADA
Storytelling

ALITHA E. MARTINEZ
Background Assists

BRIAN HABERLIN & **AVALON STUDIOS**
Colors

RICHARD STARKINGS & COMICRAFT'S **SIOBHAN HANNA** & **WES ABBOTT**
Letters

JOE QUESADA, JIMMY PALMIOTTI & NANCI DAKESIAN
Editors

Black Panther created by STAN LEE & JACK KIRBY

Collection Editor **MARK D. BEAZLEY**   Senior Editor, Special Projects **JENNIFER GRÜNWALD**   Editor In Chief **C.B. CEBULSKI**

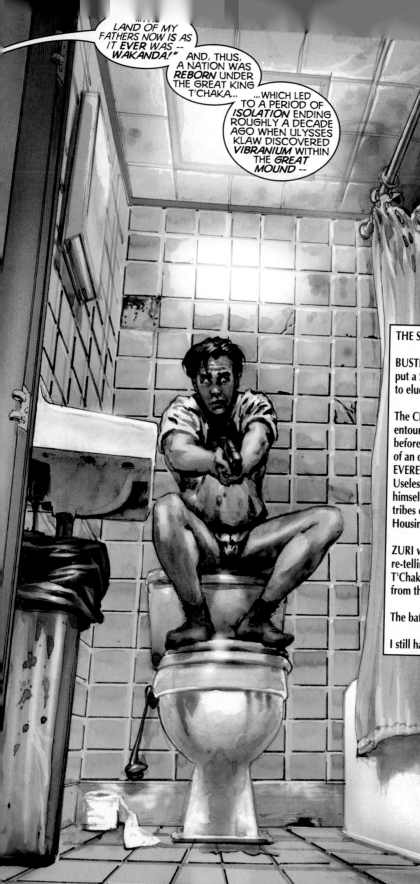

THE DEVIL.

THE DEVILTHEDEVIL THEDEVILTHE DEVIL. I MEAN THAT LITERALLY, NIKKI.

I'M LIKE *COMPLETELY* LOST NOW.

WHICH, SINCE YOU'RE MY *BOSS*, IS *BAD*, RIGHT --?

ROSS -- ALL YOU HAD TO DO IS KEEP YOUR EYE ON *ONE* CHIEF OF STATE --

WHO LIKES TO PULL ON A KITTY CAT MASK AND LEAP OUT OF WINDOWS.

YOUR REPORT'S A *MESS*, ROSS -- I NEED SOME *CONTEXT*. GO *BACK* --

OKAY --

CHEESE

THEY TOOK MY PANTS.

6975H23
MILAJE, DORA
75th Precinct
1000 Sutter Ave
Brooklyn, New York
11208-3553
16 Sept. 1998

6975H24
ZURI, NONE GIVEN
75th Precinct
1000 Sutter Ave
Brooklyn, New York
11208-3553
16 Sept. 1998

6975H25
PANTHER, THE BLACK
75th Precinct
1000 Sutter Ave
Brooklyn, New York
11208-3553
16 Sept. 1998

6975H26
ROSS, EVERETT K.
75th Precinct
1000 Sutter Ave
Brooklyn, New York
11208-3553
16 Sept. 1998

ROSS ROSSROSS ROSS... ...THIS IS LIKE WATCHING PULP FICTION IN *REWIND*. MY *HEAD* IS EXPLODING. *BACK*, ROSS -- BACK *FARTHER*. OKAY --

EVERETT K. ROSS, MIDNIGHT WARRIOR

ROSS. BACK.

EVERETT K. ROSS, SUPERFLY

EVERETT K. ROSS -- OFFICE OF THE CHIEF OF PROTOCOL, U.S. STATE DEPARTMENT.

Y'ALL BE *COOL*. JUST *CHILL*.

DON'T START NONE, WON'T *BE* NONE.

ROSS.

ALL RIGHT, ALL RIGHT. FROM WHAT I PIECED TOGETHER AFTER THE FACT, THE WHOLE NO-PANTS THING STARTED WHEN THE CLIENT WENT OUT FOR A LITTLE *DRIVE...*

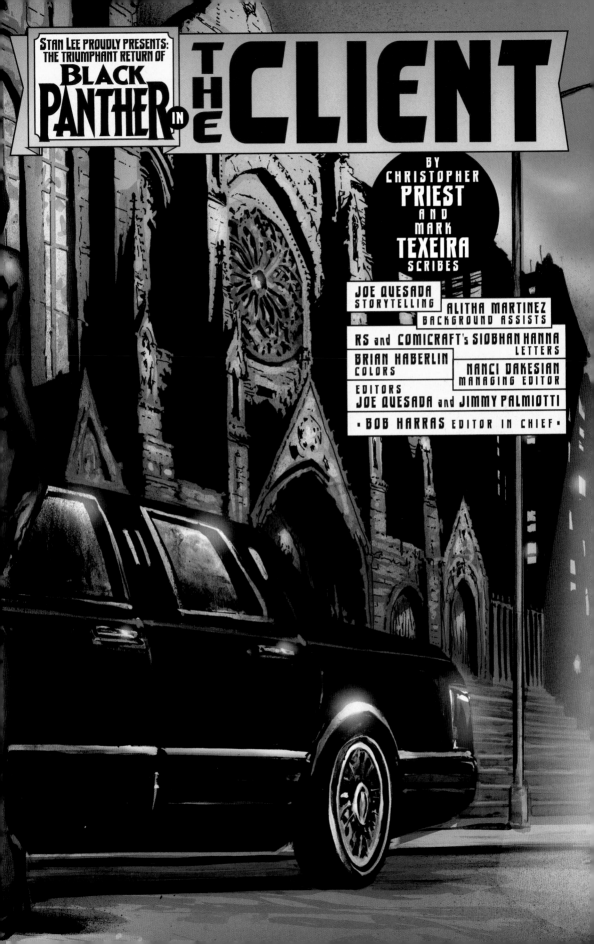

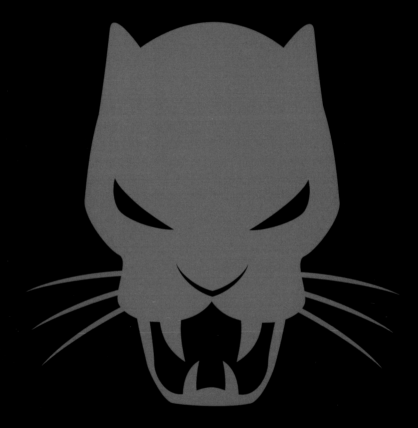

YOU THE KING OF *AFRICA*, OR SOME, RIGHT? YOU 'SPOSED TO *IMPRESS* ME OR *WHAT*?

AND WHERE'S YOUR LITTLE *CAT SUIT* -- WITH THE CUTE LITTLE *EARS*, MAN?

I HEAR YOU A *PUNK*, YO. BE CARRYIN' THEM *OTHER* AVENGERS' *BAGS* AND WHAT NOT.

"THE BLACK PANTHER." SHEE-RIGHT.

There MAY have been scarier people in town than Manuel Ramos, but I doubt it.

Ramos ran Union Local 1102 of the Fraternal Order of Cracked-Out Dope-Dealing Home Invading Sociopaths, whose front office was the south courtyard of the East New York housing project where the client, Buster and I were staying.

SO -- WHAT -- YOU AND EN VOGUE GONNA THROW DOWN?

YO, *MIRA* -- THIS IS *MY* WORLD, HOLMES. *I* BE THE KING *HERE*.

Which was why the client wanted to see him...

SAFETY YOUR WEAPONS AND LAY THEM ON THE *GROUND*.

Heh -- YOU A *FUNNY* GUY, PUSSY CAT-MAN, YOU KNOW THAT --?

The client called them DORA MILAJE, or "adored ones," and described them as the king's concomitants.

A tribal thing -- kind of wives-in-training. And a real blast at state functions.

"Deadly Amazonian high school karate chicks --? Bill Clinton. Bill --?"

OKOYE was his chauffeur, NAKIA his personal aide.

The client spoke to them exclusively in HAUSA, which made my "Swahili For Dummies" cheat book pretty useless.

The client was always reminding them that KILLING is FROWNED UPON here in the United States. He substituted some non-lethal high-tech stuff for their traditional weapons.

None of which could stop them from throwing you off a ROOF.

KEEEE

RASHHH

EY -- EYYY --!

I KILL YOU, MAN -- CUTCHO NECK --!

Wakandagate

An Avenger and African King becomes embroiled in a stateside scandal. Has the mask been lifted from Wakanda's squeaky-clean, fairy-tale like history?

The growing scandal surrounding The Tomorrow Fund exploded today, as investigators reported rampant mismanagement of funds including federal matching grant targeted for needy children in the New L section of Brooklyn, New York. While official number has been released, sou within the New York Inspector Gen office estimate as much as 17.5 milion may have been embezzled from T that TTF's accounts may have been money laundering and drug traffick

A community self-help or established several years ago, Wakandan Consulate's grant pr Tomorrow Fund's motto of Better Tomorrow" provide inspiration to thousands of youngsters, and was a hub o New York community. Inves Drug Enforcement Age Department, the FBI, an looking into the internati cash flow, and thoroug role of Wakanda, the principally responsib Fund's operationa sources report high-T'Challa, also Panther," may in despot with heav T'Challa is seen for The Tomo year-old Jam poster child.

As you kn began after murdered headqua Wakand expres anger any or c

WHICH MEANS EXACTLY *WHAT*?

DEAD KID -- SOME CREEPS MISMANAGE FUNDS -- THIS IS, WHAT, A DAY --

-- A *WEEK* OF SAM DONALDSON GRINNING WITH THAT BIG PUMPKIN HEAD OF HIS --

-- GO LONG --

-- WHY ARE YOU GIVING THIS TO *ME*? WHY DON'T *YOU* TAKE IT?

BECAUSE I DON'T *WANT* IT. YOU SHOULD BE *GRATEFUL* I'M HANDING YOU SOMETHING THIS *BIG* --

-- THIS IS A *MAJOR DIPLOMATIC INCIDENT.*

WHY -- BECAUSE THE GUY IS *BLACK*?

ROSS...

IT'S *OKAY*, NIKKI -- YOU *CAN* SAY IT -- YOU WON'T GROW *HAIR* ON YOUR BACK OR ANYTHING.

KERRAASH

THIS IS THE ONLY COUNTRY IN THE *WORLD* WHERE PEOPLE LOOK AT YOU CROSS-EYED FOR STATING THE *OBVIOUS*.

AND YOU OWE ME TWELVE BUCKS FOR THE MIRROR.

ROSS -- I'M SERIOUS -- THIS COULD BE *BIG* --

-- *KING T'CHALLA* IS CONSIDERING COMING HERE *PERSONALLY*.

NIKKI -- KING T'CHALLA IS ALSO THE *AVENGER* CALLED ELDREDGE CLEAVER --

BLACK PANTHER.

WHATEVER.

HE COMES HERE ALL THE *TIME*. HANGS OUT AT THE AVENGERS MANSION -- ORDERS UP SOME *RIBS* --

ROSS...

-- NIKKI -- THE GUY'S AS *DANGEROUS* AS *BATROC*. I MEAN, *THINK* ABOUT IT -- HE'S GOT *NO POWERS* OR ANYTHING.

I GOT THIS. NO SWEAT.

Which, of course, were my famous last words.

You see, back in Wakanda, things were a little TENSE. The client had set up a refugee camp in the kingdom's border region where tribesmen seeking ASYLUM from regional ethnic wars would be SAFE.

Safe from their governments -- but not from EACH OTHER. They kinda brought their war WITH them. The client often found himself interceding in skirmishes between the refugees, which aggravated the Wakandan people that much MORE.

See, Wakandans come pretty much in TWO flavors -- the CITY DWELLERS and the MARSH TRIBESMEN. They never agreed on ANYTHING -- until the client granted asylum to the refugees.

So, to REVIEW: the city dwellers hated the tribesmen, the tribesmen hated the city dwellers, they both hated the refugees who hated THEM in return, despite the fact Wakanda was clothing and feeding them at the time. And, of course --

-- EVERYONE resented the client because he wouldn't do things THEIR WAY.

King T'Challa was a real STRAIGHT ARROW -- an IDEALIST who became KING as a teenager after his father was MURDERED.

Educated in Europe and America, he returned home to pass a series of trials and obtain a heart-shaped herb that heightened his physical strength and natural senses.

The cat suit is largely CEREMONIAL -- it marks him as the LEADER of the PANTHER CLAN.

The client was too noble a guy to cut the refugees loose.

He determined that all of Wakanda would learn to accept one another and help their neighbors.

In other words, he wasn't much of a politician.

And that was a perfectly LOUSY time for him to hear about the Tomorrow Fund SCANDAL...

WHICH INEVITABLY LED TO MY LOSING MY PANTS...

THIS IS *FASCINATING*, ROSS, BUT I'M RUNNING OUT OF *TIME*.

THE CLIENT COMES TO TOWN -- *YOU* DUCK THE ASSIGNMENT AND GIVE IT TO *ME*. I GO TO THE AIRPORT TO PICK HIM UP. I BRING THE *MIATA*.

I figure, how much trouble could he BE?

GET DOWN JUNGLE

GET BOOGIE!

What, the guy brings a TOOTHBRUSH -- an extra pair of TIGHTS or something, right?

AIR AFRICA

SAVE IT FOR *NEXT TIME*, ROSS.

JUST TELL ME ABOUT *HIM* -- WHEN DID *HE* ENTER THE PICTURE --?

THAT'S WHAT I WAS GETTING TO --

-- THE NIGHT I WAS HUNTING BUSTER WHILE THE CLIENT WAS OUT ROUGHING UP *DRUG DEALERS* --

-- someone knocked at the door.

...AND *CONTINUING* WAKANDA'S GRAND HISTORY -- IN 1984 WE PIONEERED MAGNETIC PULSE TECHNOLOGY --

-- →HIC← --

ZURI was in his FOURTH history lesson. I thought MAYBE...if I was LUCKY... it'd be the angel of DEATH come to put me out of my misery.

JOE QUESADA & **JIMMY PALMIOTTI**
1 variant cover

THE STORY THUS FAR:

Five minutes before, I was hunting BUSTER, the Jerry Seinfeld of lower income housing rats, while listening to ZURI ramble on about the Wakandan kingdom's great history.

The CLIENT -- the king of Wakanda -- had earlier tugged on a kitty-cat mask and jumped out a window, leaving me, Everett K. Ross, America's WHITEST MAN, alone in the Leslie N. Hilll Housing Project.

Which was right when the DEVIL dropped by.

‹WE DID NOT KILL THEM, MY LORD.›

‹THERE WERE, HOWEVER, MANY INJURIES.›

The DORA MILAJE, or "adored ones," were the client's... concomitants. Soon as I know what that actually means, I'll get back to you. He spoke to them exclusively in Hausa and, as far as I could tell, they spoke only to HIM.

They were Amazonian teenage karate chicks from two Wakandan tribes. Keeping them in his family as potential WIVES somehow kept the PEACE between the city dwellers and the tribal factions of the client's kingdom.

Which, no matter HOW you looked at it, made the client the luckiest guy on the face of the Earth.

‹INJURIES DO NOT CONCERN US. REMEMBER, NAKIA, WE ARE GUESTS IN THIS PLACE.›

‹WE WOULD DO WELL TO OBEY THEIR CUSTOMS. WERE THIS WAKANDA, AND A MAN DARED RAISE A HAND TO THE DORA MILAJE --›*

‹--THEY WOULD NOW BE WITH THEIR ANCESTORS. HOWEVER --›

‹--WHEN IN ROME, WE SHALL ACT AS ROMANS.›

‹OKOYE, BELOVED -- TO THE PRISON.›

*DOR-ah muh-LAH-jay -- J & J.

PEZ --?

YOU SAY THEY TOOK YOUR *PANTS.*

-- ?!

Ah -- YES, THAT IS ACCURATE.

SO I *SEE.*

Ah... YOU... YOU'RE NOT...

...I MEAN, YOU AREN'T...

NO.

AT LEAST, NOT *TODAY.*

A *GIFT* THEN.

TO MAKE YOU MORE *COMFORTABLE* WHILE WE AWAIT YOUR MASTER'S RETURN.

-- ?! HEY --

-- HEY *THANKS* --

-- YOU CAN'T *IMAGINE* HOW --

Oh -- *DHUH* -- LOOK WHO I'M TALKING TO! I REALLY APPRECIATE --

YES I CAN.

My god. Oh, my sweet lord.

I'd just sold my soul for a pair of pants.

I was wearing the Devil's pants...

"ROSS -- *ROSS* --"

T'Challa was king of the most advanced nation of the African continent, and possibly the world. The client had been king since his late teens -- no small accomplishment in a world of revolving-door despots.

He was sitting alone, somewhere near the HOLE that USED to be a TV set, staring at a credit card. For about ten seconds he looked like the loneliest guy in the world. And then I realized he wasn't so much LONELY as he was ANGRY.

From childhood, he'd been taught to keep a lid on his emotions, and he got so good at it that you might misread restraint for indifference. The discipline was to always be one step ahead of the next guy. Being caught unawares was an indignity the client couldn't afford. And that's what that face was --

-- the quiet indignity of getting some really bad news.

ACHEBE.

A name I didn't recognize, but the splintering of the world's greatest poker face said it all.

HE WAITED UNTIL YOU'D LEFT, T'CHALLA -- SYMPATHIZERS INSIDE CENTRAL WAKANDA SABOTAGED THE DEFENSE GRIDS --

I'LL RETURN AT ONCE, MOTHER --

AND DO WHAT, T'CHALLA? FIGHT? SO MORE INNOCENTS CAN DIE?

DON'T YOU THINK THAT'S JUST WHAT HE WANTS?

HE WANTS YOU DEAD, T'CHALLA. I'M SURE HE'S GOT GOONS WAITING FOR YOU THERE IN NEW YORK.

YOUR FATHER TAUGHT YOU ALL THAT WARRIOR NONSENSE -- BUT HE ALSO TAUGHT YOU HOW TO THINK.

DON'T FIGHT THIS WAR WITH GUNS, T'CHALLA.

SO, YOUR HIGHNESS -- I TOOK THE LIBERTY OF RESERVING A COUPLE *FLOORS* AT THE *PLAZA* -- UNLESS YOU'RE HEADING OVER TO *AVENGERS MANSION* --

NO, Mr. ROSS -- WE GO TO *NEW LOTS,* BROOKLYN.

Minutes later we were cruising the Van Wyck. Somehow, I think the HIGHWAY PATROL knew we weren't Clinton.

The client's armored stretch Lexus, sent over from the Wakandan consulate, followed behind us. It was EMPTY, so as not to hurt my FEELINGS.

Riding EXPOSED like that, I kept hearing that funky Zapruder film sprocket noise while I mentally updated my resume.

Oh -- THE *TOMORROW FUND* HQ -- WANT TO GET STARTED RIGHT *AWAY,* Huh?

FINE -- JUST TELL ME WHERE TO FORWARD YOUR *LUGGAGE* --

WE SHALL *ALL* BE *STAYING* IN NEW LOTS.

Back...and to the left...

Oh, THAT'S A GOOD ONE, YOUR HIGHNESS --

-- YOU -- YOU *ARE* JOKING, RIGHT --?

Back...and to the left...

Back...and to the left...

SO, YOUR CLIENT OPTS TO SLEEP IN A *HOUSING PROJECT* OVER A LUXURY HOTEL.

RIGHT.

AND THEN YOU LOST YOUR PANTS.

WRONG. FIRST WE WENT FOR CHINESE.

THEN I LOST MY PANTS...

THE FINEST HOUR

Wow. I'd been anointed. Who knew.

FOR WAKANDA!

FOR EVERETT K. ROSS!

FOR NEW LOTS!

The client and his bookends tried to break it up, but by THAT time --

--I was kind of INTO it.

I had flashbacks of Natalie McPhail shoving me off the monkey bars in third grade. My EGO beat the snot out of my COMMON SENSE.

I lost my pants.

Just like with Natalie...

KIDS -- KIDS --

--LET'S PLAY A ROUND OF "GUESS WHO'S GOIN' TO THE POKEY."

LET'S JUST SAY IT WASN'T MY FINEST HOUR.

WHICH EXPLAINS...

6975H23
MILAJE, DORA
75th Precinct
1000 Sutter Ave
Brooklyn, New York
11208-3553
16 Sept. 1998

6975H24
ZURI, NONE GIVEN
75th Precinct
1000 Sutter Ave
Brooklyn, New York
11208-3553
16 Sept. 1998

6975H25
PANTHER, THE BLACK
75th Precinct
1000 Sutter Ave
Brooklyn, New York
11208-3553
16 Sept. 1998

6975H26
ROSS, EVERETT K.
75th Precinct
1000 Sutter Ave
Brooklyn, New York
11208-3553
16 Sept. 1998

I D.I.'ED THE A.D.A. GOT US SPRUNG, WHICH LED BACK TO THE HOUSING PROJECT. ZURI'S HISTORY LESSON* --

-- AND THE *DEVIL'S* PANTS.

THERE YOU GO.

*D.I. = Diplomatic Immunity, A.D.A. = Assistant District Attorney -- J & J.

YOU EVER BEEN ON JERRY SPRINGER --?

SO -- WHERE *WAS* THE CLIENT --?

STILL INVESTIGATING THE *TOMORROW FUND* THING.

HE DECIDED TO PAY A VISIT TO THE FUND'S *DIRECTOR* -- *AFTER* VISITING HOURS...

THE NAME

Marion Vicar had been the Executive Director of the Tomorrow Fund. After the scandal broke, she was nailed on fraud, embezzlement and money laundering. None of which concerned the client.

See, there was this child. One day, he was holding her in his arms.

One day she was dead in an alley.

And the client was a man of remarkable focus.

I WANT A *NAME*, VICAR.

-- ?! WHO --?

AAAHH!

A *NAME.* THE MAN WHO *CORRUPTED* YOU. WHO CONVINCED A DECENT AND HONORABLE WOMAN TO SUBVERT A CHILDREN'S CHARITY --

-- INTO A MONEY-LAUNDERING OPERATION FOR DRUG CARTELS. WHO CAST A *SPELL* ON YOU, VICAR?

MISTER -- Y-YOU C-CAN GO TO *HELL* --!

BRUCE TIMM & DAVE KEMP

-- before leaving with Bob's WIFE, who had fallen in LOVE with the rebel leader, the postman having rung twice.

Understandably, Bob got a little ticked off. The legend says he refused to die out of HATE. That he made a deal with the DEVIL. Now, you'd think Bob would hunt down the guerillas, killing them one by one. Nah, too easy.

Bob went after his wife's MOTHER and FATHER. Her brothers, their wives and children. Her sisters and their families. He burned all of their homes to the ground and stabbed each of them exactly 32 times.

Bob went after his wife's FRIENDS. Her TEACHERS. He worked the list. He went after every living soul his wife had ever encountered until, finally, there was NOBODY left...

BY **CHRISTOPHER PRIEST** & **MARK TEXEIRA** STORY & ART

ORIGINAL SIN

JOE QUESADA
STORYTELLING
ALITHA MARTINEZ
BACKGROUND ASSISTS
BRIAN HABERLIN
COLORS
RICH S AND **COMICRAFT**'s
SIOBHAN HANNA
LETTERS
NANCI DAKESIAN
MANAGING EDITOR
JIMMMY PALMIOTTI
AND **JOE QUESADA**
EDITORS
BOB HARRAS
EDITOR IN CHIEF

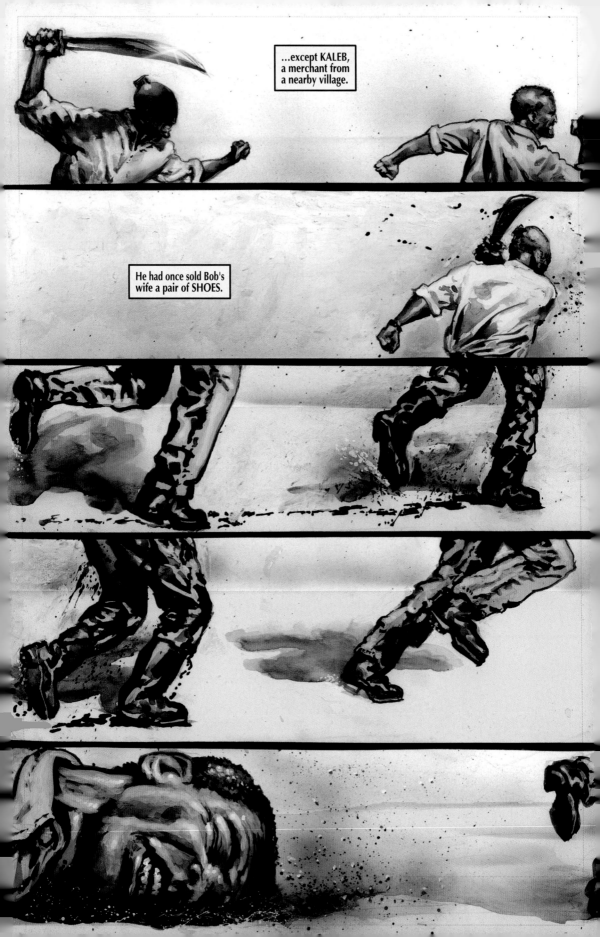

SO THE RUMOR IS *TRUE*, UKATANA. NO GOOD DEED *DOES* GO UNPUNISHED.

THIS IS A TIME OF *GREAT TURMOIL*, ACHEBE. IGNORANCE AND FEAR ARE *EASILY* EXPLOITED.

Ukatana = Zulu for "kitten"
— J & J

WHICH EXPLAINS *ME.* ERUDITION AND ELITISM ARE EVEN *EASIER* TO EXPLOIT. WHICH EXPLAINS *YOU.*

WHAT DO YOU *WANT*, CLERIC? *PEACE*, OF COURSE. AND MAYBE ONE OF THOSE NEW *MINI-DISC* PLAYERS.

THE MIGHTY UKATANA -- FETISH GOD OF THE FAT, THE SPOILED, AND THE SELF-ABSORBED.

T'CHAKA MUST BE GETTING A LITTLE *CHAFED* FROM ALL THE *360'S* HE'S TURNING IN HIS *GRAVE.*

THAT'S IT, UKAT, I'LL SELL OUT MY COUNTRYMEN FOR THE NEW WU-TANG CLAN CD, LET'S *SHAKE* ON IT.

YOU ARE *SAFE* -- YOU HAVE *FOOD* -- MEDICAL ATTENTION --

HOW RUDE OF US. TRAPPED BETWEEN THE *DEATH* IN OUR HOMELAND AND THE *PENS* HERE --

-- WE IGNORANT GHUDAZAI NEGLECT TO FALL TO OUR KNEES BEFORE OUR NOBLE SAVIORS.

YOU FOOLISH WHORES -- SO VERY CONVINCED THIS MISERY WAS SOMEHOW THE PRODUCT OF OUR OWN *IGNORANCE.*

SO *CERTAIN* YOU WILL NEVER FIND YOURSELVES IN *RAGS*, PENNED UP LIKE *ANIMALS* --

-- FIGHTING FOR EVEN THE *SMALLEST* SHRED OF *DIGNITY.*

I WILL MAKE MYSELF *AVAILABLE* WHEN YOU ACTUALLY HAVE SOMETHING TO *SAY*, ACHEBE.

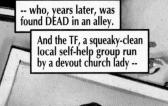

The Wakandan consulate once bankrolled a local children's charity called The Tomorrow Fund.

The client made publicity photos with the TF's poster child --

-- who, years later, was found DEAD in an alley.

And the TF, a squeaky-clean local self-help group run by a devout church lady --

-- became a BANK for local drug dealers and other lowlifes.

ALL of which was designed to appeal to the client's sense of HONOR...

...drawing him out of Wakanda so our friend BOB... ACHUBBY... whatever... could change addresses from the refugee camp to the king's palace.

The client now knew he'd been HAD.

Everything within him demanded he rush home and deal with Bob. But, as I mentioned before --

And the client had had his fill of us.

Richmond sank like a STONE, which made it harder for the client to keep up --

-- but not impossible. Thick cords of steel sinew --

Or so I imagine. I wasn't there.

Remember, I was WAITING for the guy -- making SMALL TALK with BEELZEBUB.

The soles of the client's boots were thick pads of a VIBRANIUM alloy.

Vibrating the pads at different frequencies gave them multiple uses, including running up the sides of buildings --

-- and landing from heights of 50 feet. All without making a SOUND.

-- much like my OWN -- locked up and propelled the client downward.

The DORA MILAJE were sort of wives-in-training.

⟨HAVE... HAVE I DISPLEASED YOU, MY KING --?⟩

The client always insisted that role be CEREMONIAL.

He would NEVER put his hands on them. See, in their custom, if he ever -- ah -- *closed the deal* --

⟨BELOVED STOP TH CAR.⟩

-- it would be a declaration of intent. And the girl could NEVER marry ANYONE but the king.

And, I'm not sure, but I think that was about when all the SHOOTING started...

The client was CERTAIN his enemy knew that.

Which confirmed his fear that his enemy was not so concerned with his DEATH...

...as his DESTRUCTION.

He left the girls to clear his head.

NEXT:
THE PRICE
THE SHOOTING STARTS...

The story thus far:

The client had just awakened from a hallucination to find himself kissing his secretary.

In Wakandan culture, that was as good as a proposal.

He'd left his car to go clear his head when two guys stepped out of thin air and rushed to make his acquaintance.

Meanwhile, the Reverend Dr. Michael Ibn al-Hajj Achebe, the new and self-appointed leader of the "transitional government" in Wakanda, was holding his first press conference...

This is a time of great sorrow and great sadness for the Wakandan people. In the interest of peace, and in the absence of the king, I have with great reluctance stepped forward to serve this nation...

...in prayerful hope that I, as neutral arbiter, may prevail upon the parties that a military solution will not provide a satisfactory outcome.

Let us pray...

There is some good news to report, my brothers. Though much of the Ghudazai resident subdivision was destroyed in the fighting...

...rescuers DID manage to save Muatu here! Though wounded, doctors assure me, Muatu will indeed make a full recovery! See? Things are getting better already!

The minute he got a glimpse of his attackers, the client knew the 313 rounds of spent ammunition and multiple bone fractures were just the embossment on the dinner invitation.

He was being SUMMONED. By someone he'd known all his LIFE...

...and hoped he'd never see AGAIN.

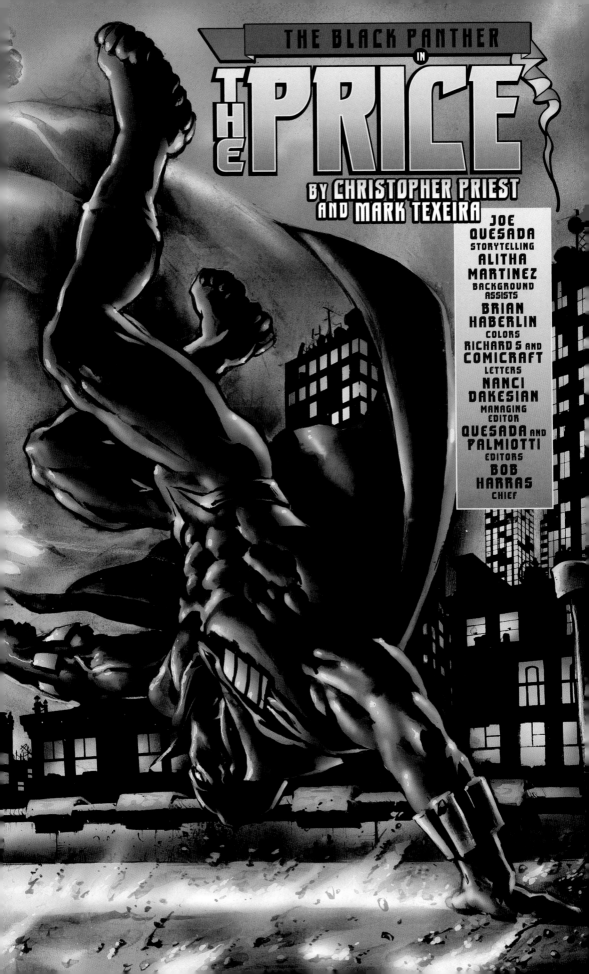

The two guys were called Hatut Zeraze.

The DOGS of WAR.

T'CHAKA, the client's late father and former king of Wakanda, certainly COULD have had lots of button men squirreled away in dark corners.

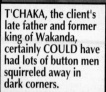

BRRATTATTATT

The way the client explained it to me, the closest analogy would be Wakandan SECRET POLICE.

Of course, Wakanda HAS no secret police. Well, so far as OCP knows, anyway.

Though, I guess, they could be SECRET.

But they aren't around anymore.

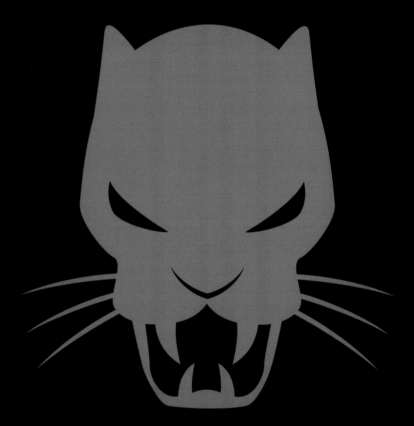

HEE HAW WAS NEVER LIKE THIS

KENNY

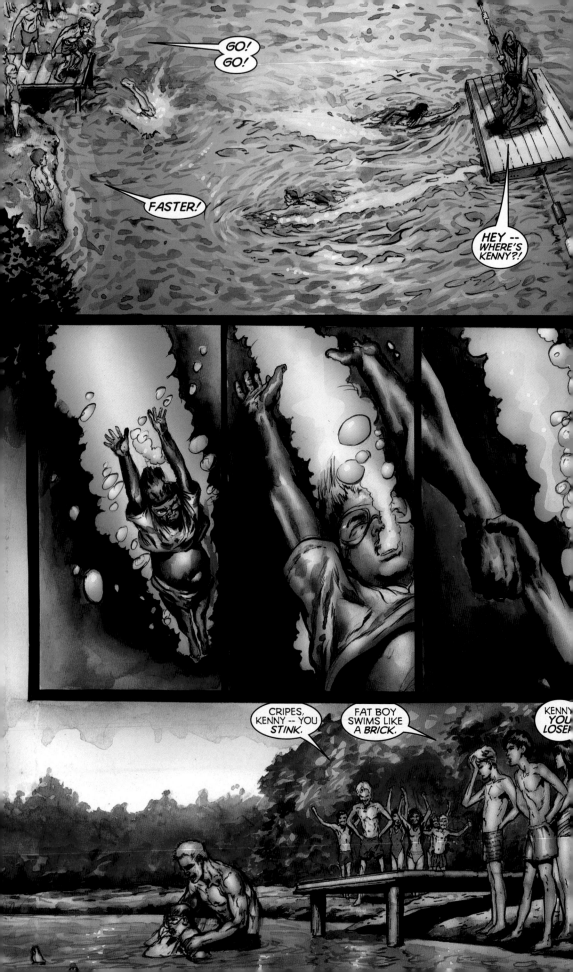

-- well, who knew, but most of them were tech types, some of the most brilliant minds in Wakanda. Panther's entourage had taken over two abandoned floors in the housing project. They'd been MONITORING Mephisto. They already KNEW he drew his power from whatever dimension he came from, and they had an idea how to cut the circuit.

See, whether MYSTIC or SCIENTIFIC, Mephisto's powers -- like everyone else's -- depend on a certain set of constants, like gravity, atmosphere and molecular cohesion. Change ANY of those constants, and the magic isn't quite so magic anymore.

Defeating Mephisto was a simple matter of changing the molecular constant of the universe, which was accomplished simply enough --

-- by placing a personal FORCE FIELD around Mephisto, and remodulating the field thirty times a second.

MAYBE that bought the client eight seconds of confusion.

He only needed THREE.

SSPLUGGSSHH

...but I think that's about where everything went to HELL...

NEXT:
THE ORIGIN OF THE BLACK PANTHER
PLUS: ROSS GOES TO HELL

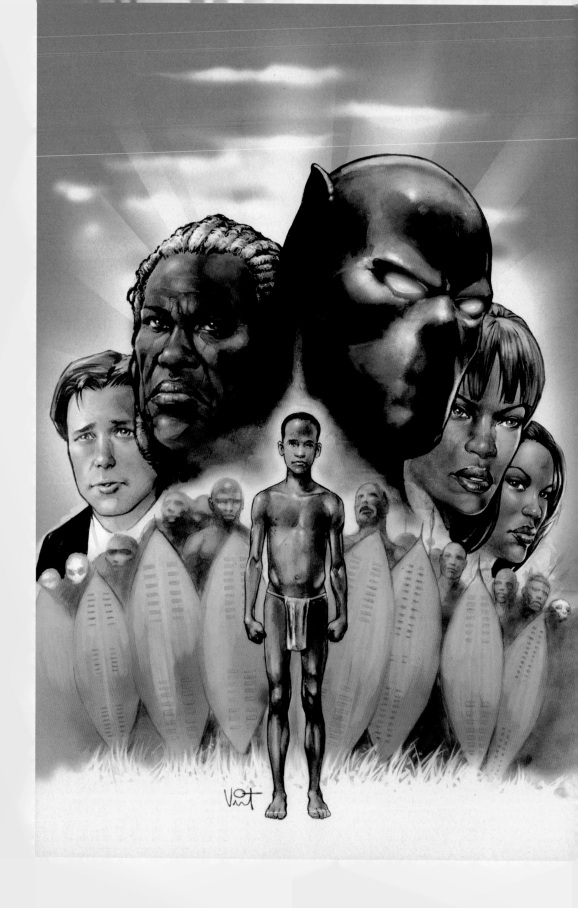

STAN LEE PRESENTS: THE BLACK PANTHER

LORD OF THE DAMNED

CHRISTOPHER PRIEST STORY VINCE EVANS GUEST ARTIST
BRIAN HABERLIN COLORS RICHARD STARKINGS AND COMICRAFT'S WES ABBOTT LETTERS
NANCI DAKESIAN MANAGING EDITOR PALMIOTTI AND QUESADA EDITORS BOB HARRAS CHIEF

The story thus far:

AAAAAAAAAAAAAAA
AAAAAAAAAAAAAAA
AAAHHHHHHHHHHH
HHHHHHHHHHHH!!!

He was talking about Mephisto's HEART, in a jar next to the Chinese take-out.

HEY--! ANYBODY ALIVE IN THERE--?!

ZURI was a close friend to T'CHAKA, the client's father and former king. He was kinda like George Clinton without the rhythm. A tribal Uncle Fester, if you will. He'd been sleepin' so long I assumed Mephisto had used his powers on him.

HIYA, JEHOVAH'S WITNESSES.

WHERE'S THE KITTY?

IF YOU ARE REFERRING TO MY MASTER, HE HAS NOT YET RETURNED.

BUT YOU EXPECT HIS ROYAL FANCY-PANTS? MIND IF I HANG OUT?

WHAT YOU DO IS IRRELEVANT TO ME, INSECT.

THAT'S SERGEANT INSECT, PALLY.

...GRUMBLE... MUST BE SOME-THING TO EAT IN THIS ACCURSED PLACE...

LOOKS LIKE THERE'S SOME OF THAT CHINESE TAKE-OUT IN THERE*

CRIPES...HOWYA GET WHEEL OF FORTUNE ON THIS THING...

*NYPD Sgt. Tork met Panther and Zuri at a Chinese restaurant in issue #2 -- J&J.

AND, GEEZ, WHO THE HUMPTY-DUMPTY IS THIS GEEK--?

THAT IS A DEAD MAN --

-- THE MOMENT I GET MY HANDS ON HIM. HIM, AND HIS SCRUFFY LITTLE DOG AS WELL. >EEEURRUPP<

FRIENDS

APOCALYPSE THEN

The ancient kingdom of Wakanda sprung up around something they called THE GREAT MOUND, which we believe is actually a fragment of a huge meteor that fell to earth thousands of years ago. Their religion evolved into a deification of the black-furred panthers they believe protected the Great Mound.

The leader of the Wakandans was a fierce warrior named T'CHAKA. Legend has it he was the greatest of ALL the Wakandan chiefs. As leader, T'Chaka took on both the name and the ceremonial garb of THE BLACK PANTHER.

Wakanda was HIDDEN from most outsiders, developing a culturally and technologically superior civilization, unspoiled by the modern world. Or at least it WAS until Ulysses Klaw came along.

FATHER--!
I MUST TELL YOU --

THE PRINCE--!
SEE TO HIM, ZURI.

--?!?
MY KING--?!

LOVE HIM AS YOU LOVE YOUR KING. THE HOPE OF WAKANDA IS IN YOUR HANDS.

Posing as an ivory hunter, Klaw was actually a geologist who'd charted the track of a meteor he believed hit Earth; a meteor he believed might have unique properties.

He'd managed a low-level reconnaissance of the mound and had been studying the properties of the ORE found within it-- something he called VIBRANIUM. It was a revolutionary metal that could ABSORB SOUND, and there was enough of it there to make Klaw the richest man in the WORLD. Klaw's backers supplied him with his own personal ARMY, and he headed off to the secret kingdom.

He tried to sweet talk T'Chaka into a deal. Y'know, "Sell me this land in exchange for these pretty fire beads."

KLAW -- THEY'RE NOT STOPPING! WE'VE GOT TO GET OUT OF HERE!

SHUT UP!

YOU'LL BLOODY WELL GET US ALL KILLED!

When THAT didn't wo Klaw went to "Plan B."

And, for a MINUTE, Klaw looked like Cus at Little Big Horn.

BLAM

But, moments later, T'Chaka looked like Sitting Bull at Wounded Knee.

Klaw called it a SOUND BLASTER. It transformed sound into powerful energy he called "solidified sound."

HHRAZZZ

Powered by conventional means, the thing was deadly.

FATHER-- --NOOO!

ZURI-- RELEASE ME! I COMMAND IT--!

I AM SORRY PRINCE --

-- SUCH IS THE WILL OF THE KING --!

Powered by VIBRANIUM...

FRUUMP

I'M...
I'M HOME --
I'M -- I'M
ALIVE --!
AND...
I HAVE NO
PANTS...

I HAVE NO
PANTS! I
HAVE NO
PANTS!

GOD, I
LOVE THIS
JOB!

Ah --
ZURI!

-- WHAT'S
THAT YOU'RE
SNACKING
ON --?

KNOCK
KNOCK
KNOCK

"..."

...Ah...

-- ?!

...MORTALS...

NEXT
KRAVEN
JUSKO
THE HUNT BEGINS...

THE STORY THUS FAR:

was so excited. Artist Joe Quesada and I had been missing each other's phone calls for a week, but I knew he wanted to talk to me about his new MARVEL KNIGHTS imprint. This was it, I thought: I was finally gonna get my dream shot. I was finally gonna get a chance to write DAREDEVIL.

I was a little horrified when the words "Black" and "Panther" came out of Joe's mouth. I mean, Black Panther? Who reads Black Panther? Black Panther?! The guy with no powers? The guy in the back of the Avengers class photo, whose main job was to point and cry out, "Look — A BIG, SCALY MONSTER! THOR — GO GET HIM!!" That guy?!

No, PANTHER was not the move. Panther was, by most any objective standards, dull. He had no powers. He had no witty speech pattern, bub. His supporting cast were a bunch of soul brothers in diapers with bones through their noses. King T'Challa is, by necessity, a man of secrecy and cunning, which is difficult to illustrate if he has thought balloons over his head telling the reader everything he's thinking. Or, worse, if he's narrating his own story and blathering on and on and on. Hard to convey cunning from a motormouth.

Also, Panther was a black super hero, and the most basic economic lesson this business can teach you is minorities and female super heroes do not sell (but kudos to Marvel for trying to do both with the black female version of Captain Marvel).

But Joe and his partner, inker Jimmy Palmiotti, were adamant: the book can work, they insisted. If we have a fresh approach, perhaps along the lines of Eddie Murphy's *Coming To America*, where the crown prince of an African nation comes to America in search of a bride. Given that kind of energy, taking Wakanda and the Panther seriously, and concentrating on how people react to him — that approach might have a chance in the market. Get him out of the jungle. Bring him to Brooklyn. Make him a night creature, a fearsome African warrior, a manner of black man most blacks in Brooklyn have never seen.

Nah. I was still unconvinced. "Look, guys, we're talking about a king. A black king of not just an African nation but a powerful nation with advanced technology capable of posing a threat to U.S. national security. A king who is prone to occasionally leaping out of windows dressed in a kitty cat outfit. If this guy, and his nation, actually existed, there's just no way the U.S. State Department would let this guy wander around unescorted, and the CIA would be constantly trying to figure out what's going on in Wakanda. There'd be all manner of global and domestic and racial politics involved."

For me to flesh out Joe and Jimmy's PANTHER premise, I'd need to go to the wells of snarkdom, for the snarkiest snark I was capable of. Social politics as interpreted by Richard Belzer or Dennis Miller. And Marvel hasn't been the home of true snark since they sent Steve Gerber and his duck packing. I was trying to chase Joe and Jimmy away, but this stuff just excited them.

Again and again I whined, There's no way Marvel would let me write this. It's a violation of the Fantasy Land Nice-Nice Accords, signed by both DC and Marvel, that says the U.S. government is always good all the time, everyone accepts Panther, and the Avengers hold hands and sing and what have you. Mainstream comics were demented places where heroes actually referred to themselves as "heroes," and villains as "villains." These were places run by people who have run comic book companies far, far, far too long and have completely lost touch with popular culture or with what young people today are actually about. I have had my hand slapped more times than I can count for simply pointing out the absurdity of what we do -- all these colorful men and women who fly around wearing their underwear on the outside of their clothes.

I believe Chris Claremont was the first writer who made sense out of all of this for me when he humanized the deadly Magneto. Claremont's brilliant writing had some of his heroes acting in completely unheroic ways, and he presented many of his villains as conflicted, desperate souls who never, ever, referred to themselves as "villains," and certainly never thought of Xavier and his ilk as "heroes."

Frank Miller and others followed suit, bringing more dimension and plurality to the Marvel Universe (while, for the most part, DC continues fairly entrenched in a kind of whitewashed estrangement from the real world, nearly all their heroes being beloved, respected and trusted by the average citizen, to whom flying men and women are a mundane and accepted practice).

The PANTHER book Joe and Jimmy were asking me to produce could not possibly exist in such a world. It would have to exist on the fringes of that world, with our book regularly hacking chunks out of it. This was fine with the guys, and they both encouraged me towards my darker side; the wittier and more gleeful the discourse, the more they enjoyed it and the harder they fought for it.

The problem with race and popular media is, in most every "black" movie or "black" music you'll see or hear, there is some hostility directed towards whites. Now, were I a white male, I certainly wouldn't want to spend eight bucks to go see a film where white males are portrayed as stupid and are the butt of every joke, or where I am made to feel guilty about things I had nothing to do with, or prejudices I don't actually have.

That's my pet peeve with a lot of black films and comedians: it's all White People Bashing, fueled by our race's legacy of anger and resentment by centuries-old unreparative wrongs. But this hostility polarizes rather than unites. There is no healing in it, and it limits our opportunities.

I feel the most profound statement I can make about race is to make Panther so cool he transcends the racial divide here in America. Rather than try and force the readers to identify with a black character, I accepted the fact a great many readers would not be able to overcome the race thing, and withdrew Panther from the reader entirely.

Borrowing a page from my mentor, legendary comics writer Denny O'Neil, I reinterpreted T'Challa in the mold of Denny's brilliant Ras Al Ghul, a villain from Batman's glory days. Nobody, not even Batman, ever knew, for sure, what Ras was thinking, what his true motives or true plans were. He was the world's greatest poker face, and only the legendary Darknight Detective had the power to challenge him. Ras was, like O'Neil himself, cool. And his coolness transcended race, gender, and even Ras' advanced age.

That was the energy I wanted for Panther. Rather than get into his head with a forced intimacy that worked against his stealth, we withdrew altogether, pushing him to the shadows and, to some complaint, making him almost a guest star in his own book. Only, in any reasonable analysis of the series, Panther clearly drives the book. Even if he has only a handful of lines per issue, he is the dominating force.

So, how do we do a book about a black king of a black nation who comes to a black neighborhood and not have it be a "black" book? Moreover, how do we deal with reader apathy and resistance to the return of one of Marvel's least appreciated and dullest characters? Do we turn Panther into WolverPanther? Do we kill him off and replace him with some kid with a crab on his face? Cut off his hand and replace it with a hook?

The answer came to me while watching the brilliant Matthew Perry perform a scene in the NBC hit sitcom *Friends*. "Gum would be perfection," a line only *Friends* fans would know, made me howl with laughter for days. Perry's character, an investment banker named Chandler Bing, was actually quite competent at his job. Respected and successful, Bing nevertheless was the horrified fish out of water when caught up in the machinery of his friends' complex personal lives. This was a role Perry freely adapted for the largely ignored but very funny film *Fools Rush In*, where he plays a brilliant corporate developer who is nonetheless The White Boob around Salma Hayek's Latino community.

I asked Joe and Jimmy, "What if we put that guy — Chandler Bing — into the series? He could be the motormouth, he could give voice to the skeptical readers and validate their doubts and fears about the series. And, best of all, he could amplify the Panther's mystery and overall enigma as his monologues would be, at best, a guess about Panther's whereabouts and motives.

The guys loved the idea, and we started hammering away at the details. This character's name was, literally, Chandler for the first couple of weeks, until I settled on an Alex P. Keaton vibe in Everett K. Ross. Most fans assumed him to be a one-off of Michael J. Fox, and Fox could certainly bring him to life, but I was writing Chandler, not Alex. I had Ross appear in KA-ZAR #17 as a warm-up of sorts, a run-through with the quick-witted, sardonic half-pint, who effortlessly got Ka-Zar off on an attempted murder charge.

With Ross in place, the book began to take shape. Ross became the key to making the book work. He was the voice of the average Marvel reader, who no doubt wondered why Marvel was bothering with another Panther series.

Ross's monologues began to steal the show, offsetting the mysterious night creature, the man of few words whom Ross was attached to. The monologues were oft outrageous, with Ross interpreting the Marvel Univer through his Everyman's eyes rather than through the ey of someone who's been reading comics all his life. It was new voice, one seemingly hostile toward the Marv Universe (and, by extension, its fans), but actually, th intent is more to be a social observer and deconstructionis

Rather than ignore or run from the looming shadow skepticism and low expectation, Joe and Jimmy and turned that stuff into kindling for the fire; the secr skepticism of most every Marvel reader became grist f our humor mill, as Ross blurted out what many fans wer likely thinking, but never dared to so much as commit t paper or post on a newsgroup: questions of race and value and our own insecurity about being super-hero fans we into adulthood. Ross giddily makes salad of all of th anxiety of the adult super-hero fan, kicking over many sacred cow in the process.

Panther's ethnicity is certainly a component of the series but it is not the central theme. We neither ignore it no build our stories around it. One of Joe and Jimmy's earlies battles with Marvel was to get the Politically Correc handcuffs off and allow us to poke fun at race (in issue # Ross assumed Panther's going to 'hang out at Avenger Mansion and order up some ribs').

That was the scene that would tell us whether Marvel wa: prepared to allow us to do this book. And, once J&: convinced the powers-that-be to leave us alone, it opened up a floodgate of possibilities for outrageous adventure and a gleeful evisceration of some of the most cherished tenets of the Marvel Universe. Jimmy and Joe were regularly summoned to the principal's office and kept after school for our Don Imus/David Letterman snark-fest (calling the Avengers "Gaudily Dressed Fascists," and wondering, "Who appointed them to 'avenge' me?! I don't need any 'avenging'!").

Which is how the book achieved its small cult following. The core die-hard PANTHER fans regularly tune in not so much for the super-hero battles or the villain of the month as to see what Ross will say about it.

To the great surprise of most industry experts, and even to myself, BLACK PANTHER is, at this writing, still going strong. Still attracting new fans and pursuing new adventures. We're thrilled and grateful to everyone who's been along for the ride. To old friends and new: to Joe, Jimmy and Nanci, to Chris Claremont who fought the good fight, to Bob Harras who often beat up Chris for us, to our pal Ruben who brought us back into the family, the great Tom Brevoort who took us to the next level, our new pal Michael Marts, to Bill Jemas for being in our corner when it really counted, the wonderful Alitha Martinez without whom we'd have NEVER shipped on time, to colorist Brian Haberlin, letterers Siobhan Hanna and Richard Starkings (who spent many an hour with me on the phone designing the look of Panther's graphics), and the fabulous Mark Texeira — thanks, everyone, for this ground-breaking comic. And for those who are meeting the Panther, Ross and the gang for the first time — enjoy!

Christopher Priest
JUNE, 2001

MARK TEXEIRA
3, page 18 layout & art

MARK TEXEIRA
3, page 19 layout & art

MARK TEXEIRA
4, page 4 layout & art

VINCE EVANS
5, page 1 layout & art

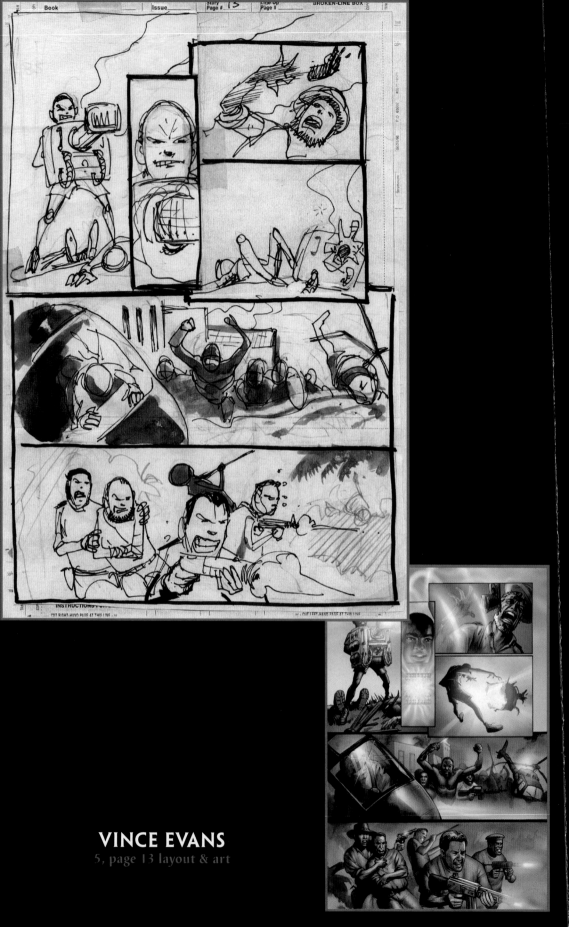

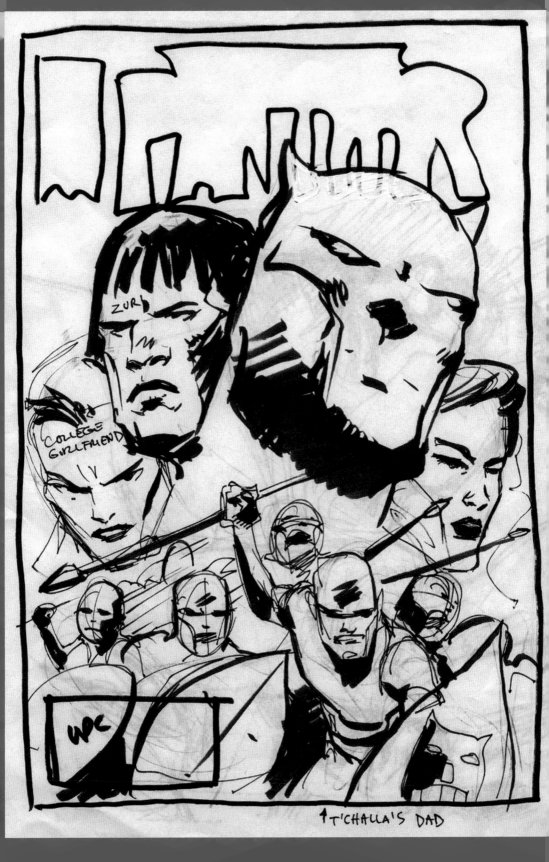

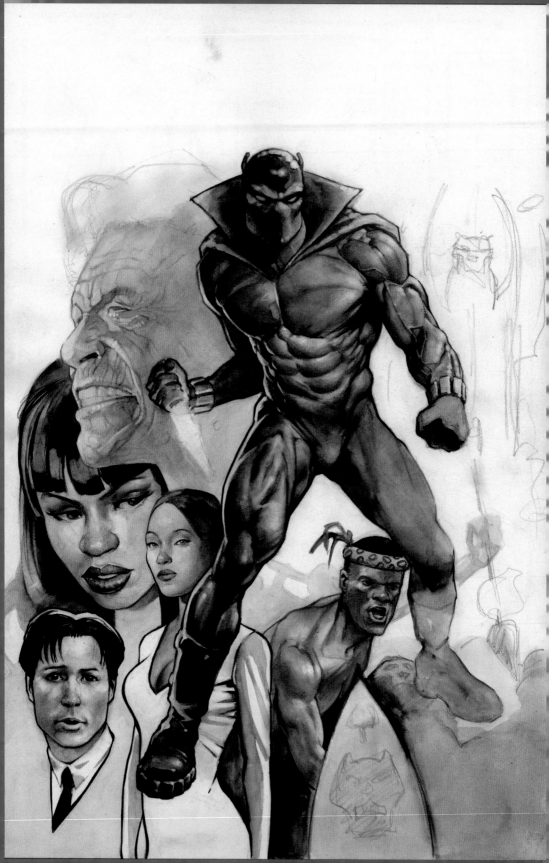

CHRISTOPHER PRIEST ON:
BLACK PANTHER

The Black Panther is *the* iconic superhero to the African-American community, and I feel especially flattered that Jimmy and Joe thought of me for this project. As reward for this starry-eyed optimism, Tex and I have turned the Panther concept on its ear with *Quantum and Woody*-levels of verve and irreverence, producing a dynamic, unexpected *Panther* book designed to cause creative whiplash for most anyone expecting, well, more of the same. We're inclusive and respectful of the Panther's proud legacy while forging new ground with a chainsaw and a blowtorch, giddily skewering the Panther's undeserved also-ran status and driving up the blood pressure of the Marvel honchos in the bargain.

Paul Schiraldi

33 YRS OLD

LENSES IN MASK GIVE NIGHT VISION TO TRACK ENERGY DAGGERS..

KIMOYO CARD : (INSERTED IN GLOVE)

CLAWS.. (ABSORBES SOUND FOR STEALTH.

<VIBRANIUM> STEEL CLAWS: EXTEND FROM FINGER TIPS. ..' NOT - KNUCKLES ..

ENERGY DAGGER ENDLESS

14

MARK TEXEIRA ON:
BLACK PANTHER

Ever since I came across artist Jim Steranko's version of Panther back in the early run of *Avengers*, I've always had an itch to try my hand at making a mark in the Panther legend. With much frustration and white-out, I've managed, with the help of Joe and Jimmy, to sculpt a formidable, fearsome image of a new '90s Panther. A kick-ass, don't-mess-with-me, take-no-crap, smack-your-mother-down-the-stairs, punch, drag-out, crack-is-whack, baddest Panther in recent history.

PROJECT: PANTHER:

KIMOYO CARD:

WHITE CONTACT LENSES, UNDER CLOTHE MASK:

TEX.
5·12·98

15